THE VIETNAM WAR

WHY THE UNITED STATES FAILED

JAMES SCHMIDT
Lieutenant Colonel, U.S. Army Special Forces

WESTBOW
PRESS®
A DIVISION OF THOMAS NELSON
& ZONDERVAN

Scripture taken from THE HOLY BIBLE, NEW INTERNATIONAL VERSION®, NIV® Copyright © 1973, 1978, 1984, 2011 by Biblica, Inc.® Used by permission. All rights reserved worldwide.

WestBow Press books may be ordered through booksellers or by contacting:

WestBow Press
A Division of Thomas Nelson & Zondervan
1663 Liberty Drive
Bloomington, IN 47403
www.westbowpress.com
844-714-3454

ISBN: 978-1-9736-4176-6 (sc)
ISBN: 978-1-9736-4177-3 (hc)
ISBN: 978-1-9736-4175-9 (e)

Library of Congress Control Number: 2018911822

Print information available on the last page.

WestBow Press rev. date: 03/07/2024

CONTENTS

DEDICATION

This book is dedicated to the men and women around the world who risk their lives for Jesus Christ and the gospel.

ACKNOWLEDGMENTS

I would like to express my appreciation to my mother, Billie Schmidt, for keeping the letters I wrote home before I was married during my first tour in Vietnam, and to my wife, Joyce, for keeping the letters I wrote home to her during my second tour. Without these letters I would not have been able to recall half of the events that took place over fifty years ago.

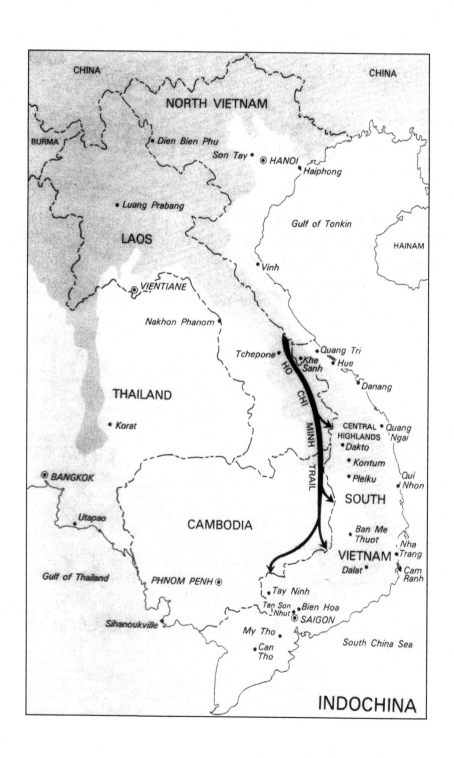

INDOCHINA

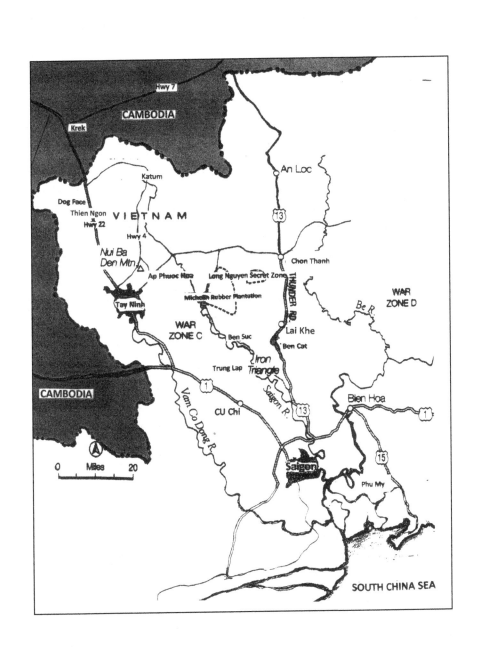

INTRODUCTION

There are some who think the war in Vietnam was unwinnable and the United States should not have fought there. This book will show that their belief is based on a lack of knowledge of military strategy and the threat communism presented. The following chapters will provide convincing evidence that the war was justified and that if it was in God's will, the United States could have had a lasting victory in the Vietnam War.

Irrespective, of America's leader's political reasons for fighting in Vietnam, America's official reason, which was to stop the spread of communism and to defend South Vietnam's freedom, was honorable and justified. This book proposes that God denied the United States victory not as punishment for fighting this just war, but to discipline America for the disintegration and decay of the nation's moral ethics, and its elected civilian leadership's self-serving motives. As a father disciplines his children because he loves them, God disciplines us out of love so that we will repent and return to Him.

As one who has led and directed men into battle numerous times, I can attest to the validity of Proverbs 21:31, "The horse is made ready for the day of battle, but victory rests with the Lord."[1] I have found that regardless of how strong one's military is, the outcome of the battle remains in God's hands. To not believe in the overruling power of God, has led to the downfall of many nations.

Throughout history God has disciplined nations for their sins, in order to persuade them to repent and return to Him. Consequently, it is my belief that out of love God allowed America to be defeated in Vietnam in order to bring us back to Him. If we as a nation expect to be successful in the future, we must not ignore God's discipline. Proverbs 13:18 gives the following warning, "He who ignores discipline comes to poverty and shame, but whoever heeds correction is honored."[2]

Military Tactical Wisdom

In the first chapter of this book, I mention a number of actions that could have contributed to victory if God had provided our civilian and military leadership the wisdom to implement them. However, most of these actions have already been discussed and analyzed by other authors; therefore, this book primarily focuses on the one area that could have led to victory, but has been overlooked. This overlooked area is ground infantry tactics. Even with the numerous self-imposed restrictions and other mistakes that were made by our leaders, a lasting victory for South Vietnam and the United States still could have been achieved if better ground tactics were employed.

The success of a strategic plan depends upon how well it is executed. Therefore, the effectiveness of overall United States strategy in Vietnam was significantly influenced by ground tactics at the military company and battalion level. This book will show that God denied American senior military leaders the wisdom to use the correct ground tactics to execute their grand strategy.

All good leaders and managers know that one cannot develop the solution to a situation without first understanding the problem. It was vital for the leaders developing military strategy in Vietnam to understand the problems that infantry units were having where the rubber hit the road. This book suggests that Generals Westmoreland and Abrams never fully understood the problems US conventional infantry units had fighting in Vietnam's jungle environment and, as a result, employed incorrect tactics.

This book is divided into two parts. Part I addresses why and how God denied victory in the Vietnam War to the most powerful country in the world. Part II describes, in chronological sequence, how God blessed the infantry company and task force I commanded in Vietnam with wisdom to use tactics which led to success and protection.

The experiences of my first tour in Vietnam (August 1966 to August 1967) had a profound influence on my understanding of both men and of tactics, so I've included many accounts of them throughout this book to complement the descriptions of operations during my second tour (May 1970 to May 1971). I hope to show how God used earlier events in my life to prepare me for what He wanted me to accomplish later in life for His honor and glory. The good and the bad tactics I experienced during my first-tour provide support for my positions on various concepts and help explain why I employed the tactics I did during my second tour.

Military scholars may find value in the identification of both failed and successful tactics; however, my goal is not to teach military theory, but to provide support for the hypothesis that the Vietnam War could have been won if God had provided the necessary wisdom to senior US military and civilian leaders.

Unfortunately, most history books fail to acknowledge our dependence on God's overruling power. Realizing that God has sovereignty over the universe, I first identify in this book why God allowed the United States to fail, and then provide evidence that the way God influenced the US failure was to deny our senior leaders the wisdom to use the correct ground tactics. Only when we include God in our study of history can we prevent repeating the same mistakes. Proverbs 1:7 states, "The fear of the Lord is the beginning of knowledge, but fools despise wisdom and discipline." [3]

Because the US failed to win a lasting victory, some believe that nothing was gained from the Vietnam War. However, if the Soviet Union was convinced that we would not interfere with their master plan of supporting communist insurgencies in vulnerable countries, they would have been emboldened to quickly expand their aggression throughout the world. Therefore, our actions during the ten year Vietnam War certainly played a part in the eventual collapse of the Soviet Union.

My motivation for writing this book is sevenfold:

1. To explain why the United States failed to win a lasting victory in Vietnam.
2. To acknowledge our dependence on the overruling power of God.
3. To emphasize that it is God who provides or denies wisdom to individuals in war.
4. To stress how vitally important it is for those going into harms-way to believe in Jesus Christ as their Lord and Savior.

5. To encourage Christians to find God's purpose for their life, and then have faith that the Holy Spirit will provide the power to achieve it.

6. To urge Christians to actively challenge America's morals and to convince American citizens to re-adopt the Bible as their moral compass.

7. To give all the glory for the success and protection of my infantry company to God the Father, Son, and Holy Spirit.

I quote many verses out of the Bible in this book. We should not take them lightly, for just as God has been faithful to his people in the past, He will be faithful to us today!

PART I

Defeat

CHAPTER 1

Why Didn't Victory Go to the Strongest Military?

If my people would but listen to me, if Israel would follow my ways, how quickly would I subdue their enemies and turn my hand against their foes!

Psalm 81:13-14[1]

Many books have been written on the Vietnam War by authors such as a former president, secretaries of defense, military historians, journalists, professors, and key generals. None, however, adequately explain why the United States was unable to prevent South Vietnam from becoming communist. This book provides the answer.

In light of Proverbs 21:31, which states, "The horse is made ready for the day of battle, but victory rests with the Lord,"[2] the short answer to the above question is: because God did not allow the United States to win.

If this is true and God controls the outcome of war, then why did God allow an atheist communist regime that restricts true religious freedom to succeed in Vietnam? It would be presumptuous for me to think that I know the mind of God, or to state that I absolutely know why God denied final victory to the United States. Therefore, I'll only suggest what I believe God's reason was, and leave readers to form their own opinions.

However, I will remind readers of God's warning to the Israelites who might disobey Him: "I will set my face against you, and you shall be struck down by your enemies...And if in spite of this you will not obey me, I will continue to punish you sevenfold for your sin."³ History shows that when the Israelites disobeyed God, He allowed evil and non-believing nations to have victory over them.

First Corinthians 10:11 tells us that, "These things happened to them (Israel) as examples and were written down as a warning for us, on whom the fulfillment of the ages has come."⁴

In light of this warning from God, and of America's increasing moral decay since the early sixties, it is my opinion that God allowed the United States to be defeated in Vietnam in order to discipline American citizens so that they would turn away from their debauchery and other evil behavior. Tragically, America as a nation has been stubborn and unrepentant, thus putting the nation in jeopardy of God's continuing punishment.

This book will show that if God had provided the top brass of the US military with wisdom and insight, they would have adopted tactics that resulted in fewer casualties, and the American public would not have lost their resolve as quickly as they did. With stronger resolve America would have been willing to use its military power to enforce the Paris Peace Accord to lasting victory.

In his 1981 book, *On Strategy: The Vietnam War in Context*, Colonel Harry Summers stated, "On the battlefield itself, the Army was unbeatable. In engagement after engagement the forces of the Viet Cong (VC) and of the North Vietnamese Army (NVA) were thrown back with terrible losses. Yet, in the end, it was North Vietnam, not the United States that emerged victorious. How could we have succeeded so well, yet failed so miserably?"⁵

I believe Colonel Summers provides one of the best analyses written of the Vietnam Conflict; however, his statement that we never lost on the battlefield has led many to assume that our tactics were correct and had little adverse effect on our overall defeat. It is true that we were always able to drive the enemy off the battlefield, but that fact in itself does not necessarily mean we employed the correct tactics. In contrast to the enemy, the United States had overwhelming air and artillery firepower; therefore, even units employing extremely poor tactics succeeded in driving the enemy off the battlefield.

Because of the false assumption that our tactics were good, the tactics used in Vietnam have never been properly analyzed. This question has unfortunately never been asked: *if we had changed our tactics, could we have suffered fewer casualties while still inflicting the same losses on the enemy?* This book provides evidence that the answer is a resounding 'yes.'

Limited Focus of Book

God allowed the United States to make many mistakes that can be attributed to the Vietnam War loss. However, it would take volumes of books to cover our involvement in Vietnam from World War II to the end of the war in 1975. Therefore, I have limited this book to the one important area that has been overlooked by other authors, which were the flawed ground tactics used by our military.

Although, this book is focused on God's intervention in ground tactics, I believe it is also important to provide the reader an understanding of other major decisions that led to the US failure. Therefore, the following paragraphs provide a good summary of mistakes that have already been covered by other authors. However, because they have already been written about, they will not be discussed and analyzed in great detail in this book.

During World War II the Office of Strategic Services (OSS) fought in Vietnam with Ho Chi Minh against the Japanese. Members of the OSS sent word back to the State Department that Ho Chi Minh told them that since the United States never was a colonial power, he trusted the US. Consequently, if the United States would not have allowed France to return to Vietnam after World War II, Ho Chi Minh may not have gone to the communist for help and the war may have been averted.

H.R. McMaster's book "Dereliction of Duty," is an indictment of President Johnson and his civilian and military advisers. It shows that politics trumped military actions. It also identified the lack of commitment to win and a lack of military knowledge and wisdom. Therefore, this book will not repeat this already published information.[6]

Additionally, many books have been written to argue the wisdom of restricting the US's military power against North Vietnam and the United States' failure to extend the Demilitarized Zone (DMZ) or Demarcation Line fortifications along the North-South Vietnam border an additional ninety miles across Laos to the Mekong River and Laos-Thailand border.

Limiting the DMZ to Vietnam allowed the NVA to bypass US fortifications much as the Germans bypassed the French Maginot Line by invading via Belgium in World War II.

Management of air force operations was done directly out of the White House by President Johnson and Secretary of Defense McNamara. Their lack of knowledge in military strategy and their focus on domestic politics resulted in poor decisions. They stopped bombing campaigns at the wrong time and imposed unwise restrictions on the US Air Force, all of which prolonged the war and resulted in the unnecessary loss of hundreds of pilots and aircraft. Their adoption of a strategy called *graduated response* showed how naive President Johnson and McNamara were. McNamara's failures also showed that computer models used to maximize profits in business did not work the same in warfare. A corporation competes with other companies for the public's business. Therefore, business computer models identify how much a company should spend on each variable such as advertising, R&D, production, etc., at a level just enough to beat-out their competition, and thereby maximizing profit. However, in war the objective is to convince your opponent that they have no hope of winning so that they will capitulate. In war the fastest way to do this is to convince your opponent that you have overwhelming combat power and are willing to use it. Unfortunately, the graduated response strategy, only convinced our opponent that the United States did not have the will to use its overwhelming combat power against them. More detail about the failure of the graduated response strategy will be provided in the fourth chapter.

The White House refused to deny our enemy sanctuaries in Cambodia, Laos and the North Vietnamese panhandle north of the DMZ; thereby, allowing our enemy's troops to escape destruction, and to have safe supply and training areas. It wasn't until 1970 that US forces were allowed to attack these sanctuaries and by that time the US forces were in the process of withdrawal.

The shameful performance of the media probably has not been addressed as much as it should have; however, it would take another book to explain the extent of damage they caused to our war efforts against the communist. However, to provide an example of the magnitude of the media's adverse impact on the war, General Westmoreland's comments about the Tet offensive are quoted below:

The enemy's objective was to inflict a military defeat on the South Vietnamese and the Americans and to generate a public uprising by the people of South Vietnam against the Saigon regime.

The enemy's defeat was so severe that it took him four years to recover. There were no public uprisings. When the people fled from the North Vietnamese invaders, it was often described by the media as a movement to avoid our air and artillery. Most South Vietnamese units fought well, but it was not the *in thing* in media circles to say anything good about the South Vietnamese. The media misled the American people by their reporting of Tet, and even a number of officials in Washington were taken in.

There is an old military axiom that *When the enemy is hurting, don't let up, increase the pressure on him.* Despite military advice to the contrary, our political leaders decreased the pressure on the Hanoi regime and enticed the enemy to the conference table. There they sat in Paris for over four years and decided one thing only – the shape of the conference table. Our official and unofficial actions provided no incentive for Hanoi to do otherwise.

To demonstrate this principle, I remind you that in 1972 after Haiphong Harbor was mined, and B-52s were used for the first time against important military targets in North Vietnam, Le Duc Tho and his colleagues came to the conference table and actually wept, saying that they could not take any more. We could have put that type of pressure on Hanoi after the defeat of the Tet offensive. The enemy would have been forced to negotiate on our terms, and thousands of lives would have been saved.[7]

A critical mistake that the US leadership made in the Vietnam War was to identify it as only an insurgency, rather than a North Vietnam invasion, that was supported by communist guerrillas in South Vietnam. By the time the US understood this, the US population and civilian leadership lost its resolve to win a lasting victory. North Vietnam propaganda that targeted opinions outside Vietnam intentionally encouraged the perception of the war as an internal conflict. Unfortunately, people in positions of influence such as college professors, government leaders, and most of the media believed the communist's propaganda; thus, unknowingly helped spread the lie. Sadly, in order to cover-up the fact that they were bamboozled, many continue to present a distorted history of the Vietnam War.

It is not clear when our senior leaders realized the true nature of the war; however, it should have been clear that after the battle the 7th US Cavalry had with the North Vietnamese Army in the Ia Drang in November 1965, that North Vietnam had invaded South Vietnam.

Communist propaganda also targeted the Vietnamese both in North Vietnam and South Vietnam. The communist's propaganda targeting the Vietnamese was to convince them that the US was the invaders, and were going to stay in Vietnam like the French had done. They seldom mentioned that their main goal was to impose a communist government in South Vietnam. Even today, if you were to ask a North Vietnamese, who had fought in the war, if he thought it was worth all the deaths, he would say that it was worth it because they drove out the American invaders and freed the South Vietnamese.

Unfortunately, the US civilian leadership was too timid to take meaningful action until President Nixon had the courage to put pressure on North Vietnam by invading their bases in Cambodia, approving an incursion into Laos, the mining of Haiphong Harbor, and expanded B52 strikes into North Vietnam. These bolder actions, and in particular the last two that were conducted in 1972, caused the North Vietnamese to finally negotiate an agreement in early 1973, that if enforced by the US would have led to a lasting victory for South Vietnam. President Nixon told President Thieu in writing that the US would fully support his military forces after our withdrawal and would react if the enemy broke the Paris Peace Accord. It should be noted that the Paris Peace Accord stated that elements of the North Vietnamese Army already in South Vietnam could stay; however, North Vietnam was not allowed to send more troops into South Vietnam.

As history shows, because the US lost its resolve, Congress passed the Case-Church Amendment to the 1974 Appropriation Act which prohibited any funds whatsoever to South Vietnam, and Congress cut military aid to South Vietnam by one-half. Finally the US committed one of the most shameful acts in America's history, the US did not react when

North Vietnam broke the Paris Peace Agreement by conducting an all-out attack into South Vietnam with thousands of troops, tanks, artillery, and equipment. In addition to allowing a nation to break a treaty with us, the US failed to honor the agreement with our South Vietnamese ally to fully support their military if North Vietnam broke the treaty. As a result of these failures, thousands of innocent lives were lost as well as South Vietnam's liberty.

I believe most military strategists would agree that if the US would have responded to the NVA invasion in 1975, by providing air support and advisors to direct US close air support to the South Vietnamese as well as B-52 strikes in both South and North Vietnam, the North Vietnamese military would have been quickly destroyed. Because NVA troops and equipment were no longer hidden in the jungle, they would have been easy targets for our air power. Additionally, breaking the treaty would have justified US B-52 strikes throughout North Vietnam.

In reality the Vietnam War was both a civil war and an invasion from outside South Vietnam's border. Knowing this, the correct strategy would be to primarily focus on defeating the invading or stronger force that is providing support for the internal insurgent. Once they capitulate then the government forces could have focused on the civil war.

Since this was not understood, for most of the war the US was primarily focused on the civil war. A civil war or counterinsurgency war is usually a protracted war and not won or lost based on the outcome of a single battle, or even on the security of the population and government. To defeat an insurgency, a government must take political, economic, military, paramilitary, psychological, and civic action. However, the most important thing the government must do is to convince their citizens that they are the legitimate ones to govern the country. After the failed communist Tet offensive it was clear that the South Vietnamese citizens, did not want to be governed by the North Vietnamese communists.

This book will reveal that the United States leaders performed many things right in fighting a counterinsurgency in Vietnam; however, two things they failed to do correctly that led to our defeat that have never been properly studied were psychological operations/information warfare and ground tactics. The US failed to convince the enemy troops and civilians that the US had no intention of being a colonial power in Vietnam as the

French, and that a communist takeover would deny them true liberty, such as religious freedom. As a result the communists were able to recruit new soldiers and motivate their troops to fight. Even though large numbers of the Vietnamese thought the US was like the French and intended to stay, the communist leadership knew all along that the US had no intention of staying in Vietnam. However, they also knew that propaganda does not need to be true, it only needs to be believable.

After the United States withdrew it was clear the United States was not like the French; therefore, North Vietnam lost its primary propaganda theme. With South Vietnam's improved counterinsurgency capabilities and with the Paris Peace Accord in place to keep North Vietnam troops out of South Vietnam, South Vietnam was on its way to victory. Additionally, after the Tet offensive, the North Vietnamese knew that the South Vietnamese did not want to be rule by North Vietnam. Therefore, the communist in the North could see that unless they broke the Paris Peace Accord and invaded the South with a large conventional force, the communists remaining in the South would be defeated. Regrettably, information and actions coming from the United States showed a lack of resolve. Therefore, the North tested the water by making a small incursion into the South. When President Ford did not bring out the B52s, they planned and initiated their major attack into South Vietnam.

Certainly, the above actions taken by the media and civilian leaders led to prolonging the war and defeat; therefore, it should be studied. However this book is written to show that even with the above identified mistakes and the disadvantages of fighting a protracted war against the communists in the Vietnam Conflict, we could still have won if the US used better ground tactics.

The next few chapters outline basic military doctrine. They also present the strategies and tactics employed by the United States and by the North Vietnamese and Viet Cong communists. These chapters will provide the background necessary to understand why some tactics and strategies worked and others did not.

The latter chapters of Part I give convincing evidence that American top brass lacked the insight and wisdom to employ the correct tactics in Vietnam. I also explain how this conclusion is based on analyses of the strategies and tactics discussed in the initial chapters. Again I remind the reader that all good things come from God, and that includes insight and wisdom.

CHAPTER 2

How God Intervenes in War

By faith the walls of Jericho fell, after the people had marched around them for seven days.

Hebrews 11:30[1]

Some people might believe that God does not approve of war, and for that reason, God does not intervene in war. There are some that also say that God only intervened in war prior to Jesus Christ's ministry on earth. They say that Jesus' Sermon on the Mount changed the old law; it now condemns all wars and those who would fight in them. As proof, they quote Jesus: "You have heard that it is said, 'Love your neighbor and hate your enemy.' But I tell you: Love your enemies and pray for those who persecute you, so that you may be sons of your Father in heaven."[2] However, the use of this verse to support the position that all wars are wrong is incorrect.

First of all, Jesus never claimed that it was God who said in the Old Testament that one should hate his enemies. Secondly, as a soldier doing his duty, I had to kill enemy soldiers many times. However, I can truthfully say that even though the enemy's mission was to kill my men and me, I never killed out of hate or revenge. In fact, killing out of revenge and hatred only interferes with clear-headed thinking; therefore, it is counterproductive in war. Finally, there is a vast difference between killing and murdering, just as there is a vast difference between a just war and an unjust war.

We should not condone the North Vietnam and Viet Cong military aggression against South Vietnam during the war; however, I believe God does want us to forgive them. Additionally, even though the communist now are in control of all of Vietnam, I think God wants us to love all the people of Vietnam and to pray that they, to include their leaders, will hear and believe the Gospel of Jesus Christ.

A Just War

To help define a just war, the Chief of Chaplains of the Army published an article in 1982. The views within the article were not necessarily those of the Department of Defense, but they are views on war by very influential individuals.

The view of St. Augustine on war (as stated in the article) is provided below:

> It was St. Augustine writing in the 5th Century A.D. that provided a moral justification for a Christian fighting in a war. Although St. Augustine would not avail himself of the natural right to repel force by force, he did concede to other men the right of self-defense. However, the moral formula was transformed even for him once a third party was introduced. He reasoned that if he were traveling upon the desert in the company of women and children and they were attacked by brigands, unselfish love for others would this time demand that he sacrifice himself in defense of the innocent victims of unjust attack. He would fight, and if necessary, die to defend them. Resorting to violence under this circumstance was seen as not only serving justice, but as a work of charity. Augustine's logic has dominated Western thought concerning the just and unjust use of force.
>
> The reasoning of St. Augustine enables us to understand the ambivalence experienced in reflecting upon war and upon the profession of arms. For St. Augustine, war was the result of sin; terrible evidence of the disorder of human existence. But war, when viewed as an essential act taken

to protect the innocent from an unjust attack, was not the result of the defenders' sin, and, therefore, was not to be considered evil. Hence, under severe necessity, war could be the lesser evil and the morally preferred act. In a sense, because good and evil were inextricably intermixed in man, St. Augustine regarded war as being at once a result of sin and a cure for sin.[3]

Although the Chaplain's article includes the views of numerous important religious and non-religious individuals throughout history, from 400 BC to AD 1982, I believe the words of Martin Luther in the sixteenth century are the most succinct summary of the issue: "A defensive war is the only true just war, and any war should be fought in the fear of God."[4]

It is not murder when a soldier takes the lives of enemy soldiers in order to stop armed aggression against one's own or another's country. This is a just war. On the other hand, it is murder when a soldier or non-soldier intentionally takes the life of a civilian or soldier of another country that is not threatening his nation or someone else's nation by armed force, and takes that life due to hatred, revenge, greed, a quest for power, or a desire to impose his own religion on others.

A war fought to defend one's innocent fellow citizens or another nation's innocent citizens from unjustified armed aggression is justifiable. Consequently, it was just to defend the South Vietnamese from armed aggression by a communist government outside South Vietnam's borders.

While for me, South Vietnam's freedom to worship Jesus Christ was cause enough to fight and risk my life, it was also critical to our national security to keep Southeast Asia non-communist. Unfortunately, many Americans did not understand military strategy and what the consequences of a communist Southeast Asia would be during a war with the Soviet Union or China. Therefore, they did not believe the United States had any business fighting for a country halfway around the world.

President Johnson deliberately did not mobilize the American people for fear of adversely impacting his Great Society program. As a result, most Americans were never told how important it was to keep the Strait of Malacca open to US ships and to have access to air and naval bases in Southeast Asia during wartime.

Additionally, although South Vietnam, Laos, and Cambodia were not members of the Southeast Asia Treaty Organization (SEATO), because of the domino threat of communism, all three countries were brought under the protection of SEATO. Therefore, the US had an obligation to defend South Vietnam from an outside attack.

Conflicts Other Than War

Even though the wars on terrorism and drugs did not have a bearing on the Vietnam War, because they are current threats to the United States, I will briefly address my thoughts on how the issue of a just war applies to them.

As defined above, a just war occurs when a nation's military fights to protect its citizens from being killed. Surely, the United States would be justified in destroying an enemy who was firing missiles into our cities and killing our citizens.

An organization that produces illegal drugs or train terrorists within the borders of a foreign country, but then sends the drugs or terrorists into our cities, is just as deadly. If the government of countries from which these deadly organizations produce their deadly product or train terrorist is unwilling or incapable of destroying the illegal drug crops or terrorist camps, then the US government has not only the right but a moral responsibility to its own citizens to destroy them.

Individual rights and sovereignty have their limits in our ever-shrinking world. If illegal activities in one country threaten the security of another, then those illegal activities are no longer just the internal concern of that country. Consequently, a policy of noninterference in the internal affairs of drug- and terrorist-producing countries is no longer appropriate.

In the past, a *state of war* was defined as open and declared armed hostile conflict between states or nations. Today, because of the magnitude of organized crime and terrorism, *war* is used to describe the fight against these groups as well. It is important to clarify that even though we use this term to talk about the fight against drug and terrorist organizations, the people in these groups are both common criminals and war criminals. They should not be considered soldiers or given the rights of soldiers as defined in the Geneva Convention. Additionally, they should not be given the rights of civilian criminal law, until the organization that they belong capitulates. And even then they should be tried as war criminals. (It should be noted that even a legitimate war combatant captured fighting <u>out of uniform</u> behind enemy lines is treated differently than those in uniform).

So as not to divert focus from the intent of this book, further discussion of the problem of illegal drugs and terrorism will be avoided. Readers interested in my thoughts on dealing with the illegal drugs problem can read my article "Hit Drug Lords' Center of Gravity," published in the July 1992 issue of *Army Magazine*.[5]

Service in the Military

We should note that Jesus never criticized those in the military. In fact, Jesus did just the opposite. In Matthew 8:10, a centurion tells Jesus to only say the word and the centurion's dying servant will be healed. "When Jesus heard this, he was astonished and said to those following him, 'I tell you the truth, I have not found anyone in Israel with such great faith.'"[6]

Similarly, John the Baptist did not forbid soldiering. John did not condemn men for being soldiers, as we see in Luke 3:14: "Then some soldiers asked him, 'And what should we do?' He replied, 'Don't extort money and don't accuse people falsely—be content with your pay.'"[7]

Acts 10 tells us that God was pleased with a centurion named Cornelius and that he was probably the first gentile to receive the Holy Spirit after Peter presented the Gospel of Jesus Christ to him and his family.[8]

One last comment before leaving this discussion of the justification of war: I think most people would agree with the well-known statement, *all that is needed for evil to prosper is for good people to do nothing.* If a person sees that something should be done to stop evil and he has the ability to stop it, but does nothing, that is a sin of omission.

Examples of God Intervening in War

God uses natural disasters, weather, plagues, and people themselves (their wisdom, special skills, technology, weapons, etc.) to influence the outcome of war. Certainly, the creator of the universe can do all things;

God is not limited in the ways He intervenes in war, or in any other events on earth. It is imperative for us to acknowledge God's power to intervene, and for us to call upon the Lord for help in all things.

For example, during the Revolutionary War, George Washington credited God for the safe evacuation of his troops from Brooklyn Heights, Long Island. In 1776, the British had trapped the American army and were about to crush them, which could have resulted in a disastrous end to the war. To save his forces, Washington conducted a risky night withdrawal across the East River the night before the British were to attack. A particularly heavy "black fog" covered their evacuation throughout the night. In the morning, the fog remained; it lasted longer than fog normally does. By the time the fog lifted, the last American boats were out of range of the British guns.

Ironically, when the British were trapped by the Americans at Yorktown, British General Cornwallis attempted a similar nighttime escape by boat; however, instead of fog, he experienced a tremendous storm that eliminated their chance for escape.[9]

In Israel's war against the Philistines, God used David, a small boy with a sling, to defeat the powerful, giant warrior Goliath, causing the Philistine army to retreat in fear. David had a great love for God, and because of his enormous faith, he had the courage to face Goliath. Thus, God blessed David with the skill to use a sling, and He guided the rock to its target.[10]

The following offers an excellent example of how God intervened in our Civil War. A little over one hundred and fifty years ago, the United States was engaged in the Civil War. President Lincoln knew the Bible and understood that victory rested with the Lord. During the first part of the Civil War the Union lost battle after battle to the Confederate Army. Lincoln attributed these defeats on the battlefield to the disobedience and pride of the nation. He declared April 30, 1863, to be a national day of humiliation, fasting, and prayer. The following is part of Lincoln's proclamation:

"It is the duty of nations as well as of men to own (acknowledge) their dependence upon the overruling power of God; to confess their sins and transgressions in humble sorrow, yet with assured hope that genuine repentance will lead to mercy and pardon; and to recognize the sublime truth, announced in the Holy Scriptures and proven by all history, that those nations only are blessed whose God is the Lord.

Intoxicated with unbroken success, we have become too self-sufficient to feel the necessity of redeeming and preserving grace, too proud to pray to the God that made us!

It behooves us to humble ourselves before the offended Power, to confess our national sins and to pray for clemency and forgiveness."[11]

Miraculously, after the nation prayed for forgiveness, the tide of the Civil War turned in favor of the Union Army. Within two days, General Stonewall Jackson, one of the Confederates' best generals, was accidentally and fatally shot by his own men. Within three months, the Commander of the Confederate Army, General Robert E. Lee, who was considered a brilliant military strategist, made the imprudent decision to send his troops across a mile of open terrain to attack Union troops in good defensive positions located on the high ground near the town of Gettysburg. Lee's unwise decision resulted in the Confederates suffering a disastrous defeat. After the Union victory at the Battle of Gettysburg, the war turned around.[12]

Unfortunately, unlike in the Civil War, during the Vietnam War the United States didn't have a leader that had the wisdom of Lincoln to call the nation to repent. As a result the United States never acknowledged its dependence on the overruling power of God nor did it repent of its immoral behavior at home. Although God had numerous methods of influencing the outcome of the Vietnam War, His primary one was to deny the United States military leaders the wisdom to employ the correct tactics.

Although I contribute the defeat in Vietnam to a lack of wisdom and creativity in America's senior military leaders, I am not suggesting that any of these leaders lacked faith in Jesus Christ, or that they were immoral. God allowed the very Godly and brilliant Robert E. Lee to make the very bad decision at Gettysburg in order to do away with slavery in the United States. Similarly, I believe God denied senior leaders during the Vietnam War wisdom in order to also influence the outcome of the war for His' purpose.

The senior civilian and military individuals responsible for the strategies used in Vietnam either claim the war was unwinnable or blame others for the defeat. This book will provide evidence that the Vietnam

War would have been winnable if God had provided US senior military leaders the insight, creativity, wisdom, and knowledge necessary for them to employ better tactics. The book identifies which strategies, tactics, and actions led to the United States' defeat, and which actions, if taken, could have led to victory.

It is, of course, important to study tactics that have worked in the past and established military doctrine, but it is even more important to ask God to provide us with insight, intuition, and creativity to develop new tactics and technology necessary to defeat our country's enemies in the future. The acclaimed nineteenth century military theorist Carl von Clausewitz states in his book *On War* that "History provides the strongest proof of the importance of moral factors and their often incredible effect: this is the noblest and most solid nourishment that the mind of a general may draw from a study of the past. Parenthetically, it should be noted that the seeds of wisdom that are to bear fruit in the intellect are sown less by critical studies and learned monographs than by insights, broad impressions, and flashes of intuition."[13]

Where does a military leader obtain these insights and flashes of intuition that Clausewitz writes about? As it is written in James 1:5, if you have faith and your motives are right, they come from God: "If any of you lacks wisdom, he should ask God, who gives generously to all without finding fault, and it will be given to him."[14]

The responsibility of leadership drove young King Solomon to pray to the Lord for a discerning heart to lead the Israelites. Because Solomon asked for this rather than for long life and wealth for himself, in 1 Kings 3:12, the Lord says to Solomon, "I will give you a wise and discerning heart, so that there will never have been anyone like you, nor will there ever be."[15]

In the following chapters of this book, I provide support for the claim that God did not give senior US military leaders the wisdom to employ tactics that could have won the Vietnam War.

Because I experienced the Vietnam War at the point of the spear as an infantry rifle platoon leader and as an infantry company commander, and because later in life I was a key contributor to planning US military strategy and doctrine, I provide the reader insight into the impact that poor company and battalion level tactics had on our overall strategy in Vietnam.

Additionally, the infantry company I commanded was considered to be one of the most successful infantry units in the Vietnam War. I not only identify problems in US tactics, but also provide what I believe would have been the solution to the Vietnam conflict, if God had provided our senior civilian and military leaders with the light to see it.

Contrary to former Secretary of Defense Robert McNamara's opinion that the war in Vietnam was unwinnable, I will make a strong case that the war could have been won if God had provided our leaders with the knowledge and creativity to employ the correct tactics.[16] I identify these flawed tactics as well as which tactics should have been employed instead. I also describe the most effective infantry tactics and techniques that were used in the latter years of the Vietnam conflict. These tactics and techniques are unknown to most previous authors of books on Vietnam. If these tactics had been used throughout the entire conflict, the United States would have gained enough time to achieve a lasting victory.

CHAPTER 3

Military Strategy and Doctrine

The fear of the Lord is the beginning of wisdom, and knowledge of the Holy One is understanding.

Proverbs 9:10[1]

This chapter on strategy is for those who have not had the opportunity to study military strategy. It provides enough basic knowledge of military strategy and US military doctrine for the reader to be able to question the wisdom of America's civilian and military leadership during the Vietnam War. Basic comprehension of military strategy will also help the reader to understand the reasons why US tactics failed. Finally, and most importantly, this chapter will help the reader see that the war would have been winnable, had God provided US leaders with the wisdom to employ better tactics.

Before one develops a military strategy, one must first understand the process by which a government causes another government to act in a particular way. The diagram below shows the spectrum of actions available to governments, from those with the least amount of pressure to those with the greatest:

SPECTRUM OF FOREIGN DIPLOMACY

1. *Voluntary Compliance*
2. *Coerced by Assistance*

3. *Coerced by Sanctions*
4. *Forced by Military Action*

Clearly, military action is the least preferred option, but when less forceful options fail, military action may be the only way to accomplish the desired objective. There is, however, a wide range of military actions from which to choose, such as military presence, show of force, demonstration, special operations, quarantine, blockade, and force entry.

The United States believed it necessary to use the military option *force entry* in order to convince North Vietnam and the Viet Cong to allow South Vietnam to remain an independent democratic nation. Once the decision was made to use military force, the objective should have been to accomplish the mission with a minimum of US casualties.

Even though, the Vietnam War has now been over for forty four years and all of Vietnam is now a communist nation, the United States is and should continue to encourage the Vietnam communist government to allow their citizens a more free society, and not to pursue military aggression against other countries. However, rather than using military force, our effort immediately after the war was initially to coerce by sanctions, and now to coerce by assistance. For example the communist government of Vietnam understands that it is in their best interest to have good relations with the United States for economic reasons. Therefore, if Vietnam wants to trade with the US, they need to allow more religious freedom. Although, the only Christian churches currently allowed in Vietnam are a few closely regulated by the government and can only be led by a Vietnamese, recently Franklin Graham was allowed to hold a Christian rally to a large group in Hanoi. Graham wisely, told the audience to support their government, while still presenting the Gospel of Jesus Christ. While, Vietnam officially is an atheist country, because of the demand for high-quality international education, the government has also recently allowed some closely monitored Christian run schools to be opened.

Once military force entry is chosen, military planner must develop their strategy. In discussing military strategy, one needs to be familiar with the US military's Principles of War and Counterinsurgency Principles (COIN). Knowing these principles will help the reader determine if our leaders had the wisdom to apply them in Vietnam; therefore the following principles are provided below.

PRINCIPLES OF WAR[2]

Objective. Direct every military operation towards a clearly defined, decisive, and attainable objective.

Offensive. Seize, retain, and exploit the initiative.

Mass. Concentrate combat power at the decisive place and time.

Economy of force. Allocate minimum essential combat power to secondary efforts.

Maneuver. Place the enemy in a position of disadvantage through the flexible application of combat power.

Unity of command. For every objective, ensure unity of effort under one responsible commander.

Security. Never permit the enemy to acquire an unexpected advantage.

Surprise. Strike the enemy at a time, at a place, or in a manner for which he is unprepared.

Simplicity. Prepare clear, uncomplicated plans and clear, concise orders to ensure thorough understanding.

Department of the Army
Operations Field Manual 100-5, B-1

COUNTERINSURGENCY PRINCIPLES[3]

Legitimacy is the Main Objective
Unity of Effort is Essential
Political Factors are Primary
Understand the Environment
Intelligence Drives Operations
Isolate Insurgents from Their Cause and Support
Establish Security under the Rule of Law
Prepare for a Long-Term Commitment
Department of the Army
Counterinsurgency Field Manual 3-24, 1-16

The final principle to be considered cannot be found in military manuals; it is one I developed early in my military career, and it has proven extremely useful.

In most military conflicts, the goal is to convince the opponent to surrender. It is my belief that in most cases *an enemy will capitulate when he comes to one of the three following conclusions*:

1. The cost of what he is fighting to gain is more than he is willing to pay (cost-benefit analysis).
2. He has no chance of winning the war.
3. He has no hope of winning a better bargaining position.

To develop a strategy, one must determine which of the above three approaches will convince the enemy to capitulate, as well as which approach the enemy will use against one's own country.

Although the above principle normally works with sane leaders, it will not work with individuals who no longer think in a rational manner, or individuals who know they will be killed even if they surrender because of atrocities they have committed. Hitler, Saddam Hussein, and Osama bin Laden are three examples of individuals who probably fall into both of those categories. Leaders such as these will need to be captured or killed by either their enemy or their own fighters who are rational enough to see the futility of continuing to fight.

Because leadership in North Vietnam was sane, the principle for convincing rational leaders to capitulate will be used to analyze strategies in the following chapters.

CHAPTER 4

American and Communist Strategy in the Vietnam War

As I stated in the previous chapter, it is my belief that a sane enemy leader will normally capitulate when he is convinced either that what he is fighting to gain will cost him more than he is willing to pay, that he has no chance of winning the war, or that he has no hope of winning a better bargaining position. Because the United States has such powerful military strength, North Vietnam and the Viet Cong knew they could not affect the physical ability of the United States to prosecute the war. Therefore, North Vietnam's approach was to try to convince the US that it would cost us more than we were willing to pay to keep South Vietnam non-communist.

The United States, on the other hand, had more than enough military power to defeat North Vietnam. US leadership, therefore, believed it would be relatively easy to convince North Vietnam that they had no hope of winning. However, our leaders failed to realize that to successfully persuade an opponent into believing they have no hope of winning, you must convince that opponent not only that you have overwhelming combat power, but also that you have the will to use it. For example, during the Gulf War, Operation Desert Shield certainly convinced Saddam Hussein that the United Nations forces had overwhelming combat power; however, it took Desert Storm to convince him that we were willing to use it. Similarly, in WWII, Japan didn't surrender after we used the first atomic bomb to destroy Hiroshima because they believed that after Americans saw the massive civilian casualties of the bomb, we would not use it again. As a result, we had to convince them that we did have the will to do so by bombing Nagasaki.

Although the US approach in Vietnam was to convince the enemy that they had no hope of winning, our leaders unfortunately adopted the strategy known as *graduated response*; this showed a hesitancy to use our overwhelming combat power. In *Summons of the Trumpet*, Brigadier General Dave Palmer states that the graduated response strategy was initially presented during a debate over bombing: "civilian planners wanted to start out softly and gradually increase the pressure by precise increments which could be unmistakably recognized in Hanoi. Ho Chi Minh would see the tightening pattern, the theory went, and would sensibly stop the war against South Vietnam in time to avoid devastation of his homeland."[1]

Unfortunately, gradually escalating our power led to a protracted war which not only allowed North Vietnam time to replenish their losses, but also to affect America's willingness to continue to fight.

Once government approaches are identified, the next step to developing a military strategy is to identify the enemy's *center of gravity* and develop a means to destroy it. Likewise, one must identify the center of gravity of one's own country that must be protected from the enemy.

In military strategy, the term *center of gravity* is defined by *Department of Defense's Joint Publication 1-02* as "those characteristics, capabilities, or sources of power from which a military force derives its freedom of action, physical strength, or will to fight."[2] In *On War*, Clausewitz describes it thus: "Out of these characteristics a certain center of gravity develops, the hub of all power and movement, on which everything depends. That is the point against which all our energies should be directed ... For Alexander, Gustavus Adolphus, Charles XII, and Frederick the Great, the center of gravity was their army. If the army had been destroyed, they would all have gone down in history as failures. In countries subject to domestic strife, the center of gravity is generally the capital. In small countries that rely on large ones, it is usually the army of their protector. Among alliances, it lies in the community of interest, and in popular uprisings it is the personalities of the leaders and public opinion. It is against these that our energies should be directed."[3]

The US strategy of graduated response played into the hands of the

North Vietnamese by allowing them, as stated above, not only time to replenish their losses, but also time to eventually convince the US that what we had to gain was costing us more than we were willing to pay. As Clausewitz stated, in small countries that rely on large ones, it is usually the army of their protector that is their center of gravity. North Vietnam couldn't destroy the army of South Vietnam's protector (the United States), but it could destroy the protector's resolve to provide protection.

Because in a democracy the citizens ultimately make the decisions to capitulate or to keep fighting, *our center of gravity was the US citizens' resolve.* Since US casualties have the greatest influence on the willingness of US citizens to stay in the fight, causing as many American military casualties as possible became a major objective of our enemy and one that we should have done a better job of protecting against.

One way that an enemy can expedite the process of causing an opponent to lose patience is to conduct a large operation that will result in a large number of casualties and prisoners of war (POWs). This was accomplished against the French at Dien Bien Phu in 1954. The NVA attempted to repeat this success in 1968 by overrunning and capturing the US Marine firebase at Khe Sanh, but new technology and greater airpower available to the Americans than the French had available to them at Dien Bien Phu prevented their success.

NVA leaders also claim that their attack on Khe Sanh was a diversion for their Tet offensive. Regardless of their intent, both Khe Sanh and the Tet offensive failed militarily; therefore, the communists' only option was to continue to fight a protracted war until they could kill enough US soldiers to convince the American citizens that continuing to fight the war was no longer worth the cost. Unfortunately for South Vietnam and the US, our own media's arrogance and ignorance reported to our citizens that this temporary increase in American casualties was proof that we were losing the war. Consequently, the communists' military defeats resulted in psychological victories for our enemy.

There was a correlation between the number of US casualties our citizens were willing to accept and the importance to national interests of saving South Vietnam from communism. The communists understood this correlation; they initiated an effective propaganda campaign, targeted at US citizens, to discredit the perceived dangers of a communist South

Vietnam. Their key theme was to label the war as internal insurgency rather than communist aggression by North Vietnam against South Vietnam. Additionally, they were able to cultivate the idea that the South Vietnamese government was corrupt. This smokescreen mislead many less-informed citizens within the US. It resulted in naïve college professors providing incorrect analyses of the war to their students and in the grandstanding media presenting biased news broadcasts; the resolve of US citizens was thereby weakened. Misinformation spread by professors and the media also led to increased peace demonstrations within the US; which strengthened the enemy's resolve.

Contributing to the antiwar movement was the decision of the president and the Congress to defer college students from military service. Since the policy only exempted men until they graduated, students eagerly believed the antiwar propaganda that supported their desire not to go to Vietnam because of their fear of being killed or disabled. Psychology 101 teaches us that it is easy to convince man to seek out and believe a position that supports what he wants to do or what he does not want to do. This is how human minds reduce guilt; thus, sometimes causing humans to do what is wrong rather than what is right.

Napoleon recognized the power of propaganda when he said, "There are only two powers in the world, the sword and the spirit. In the long run the sword will always be conquered by the spirit."[4]

North Vietnam's effective propaganda campaign also caused the US military to focus on a counterinsurgency strategy, thus neglecting a strategy to defeat and destroy the conventional threat that North Vietnam presented.

As previously stated, the North Vietnamese knew that the US had overwhelming combat power, but they also rightly believed we would not use it. The US had the capability to bomb Hanoi into the Stone Age; however, we were not willing to do it. Fear of China entering the war, as they had done in Korea, and humanitarian concerns influenced our decisions about how much of our power we were willing to use against North Vietnam.

The North Vietnamese leaders correctly believed that the US was willing to use its military power only to destroy military targets and military support targets. The US could not win a quick war as long as they protected their war fighting capability; this allowed North Vietnam to fight a protracted war. They knew a protracted war would work to their advantage as long as the US continued to use tactics that allowed North Vietnam to kill large numbers of US soldiers, thereby destroying American citizens' resolve. Unfortunately, the US tactic of using relatively large US ground troops to conduct *search and destroy* operations provided the enemy with enough targets to achieve their objective.

Additionally, North Vietnam's disinformation program gained momentum over time. The propaganda aimed to lower the perceived importance of keeping South Vietnam from becoming communist and to present South Vietnam as a corrupt and illegitimate government in the minds of American citizens. The United States' failure to counter the enemy propaganda or to use effective fighting tactics to reduce US casualties encouraged the communists to fight a protracted war.

With the withdrawal of US ground troops from Vietnam by early 1972, the North Vietnamese believed they had successfully defeated their enemy's center of gravity, the alliance between the United States and South Vietnam. Therefore, they chose a new center of gravity: the destruction of the South Vietnamese Army. In March 1972, North Vietnam invaded South Vietnam in a large scale conventional attack with tanks and heavy artillery. However, they severely miscalculated President Nixon's resolve and the effectiveness of US firepower when American advisors were still in Vietnam to direct it. As a result, North Vietnam suffered a major defeat and withdrew their attack.

North Vietnam had defeated American civilian resolve; however, President Nixon's resolve was not. US advisors and close air support (CAS) aircraft were still in Vietnam. Therefore, these in country US assets as well as the availability of B-52s and naval CAS, allowed President Nixon to provide South Vietnam the military support they needed. North Vietnam realized their mistake. Only after Congress restricted all funding and support to South Vietnam, and Nixon left office, did they attempt another invasion with conventional forces.

When North Vietnam signed the Paris Peace Accord, they may or may not already have been planning to break it and invade South Vietnam with conventional troops. However, I am sure North Vietnam knew that to win an insurgency war, they would have to discredit the legitimacy of the current South Vietnamese government and convince the South Vietnamese that a new communist government was more legitimate. With the US's withdrawal, the South lost its major protector; however, they gained a psychological advantage by increasing their legitimacy in the eyes of their people. The communists could no longer claim the current government was only a "puppet of the Americans," or that the United States was like the French and wanted to take over their country. With the legitimacy of South Vietnam's government strengthened, and having developed a relatively good counterinsurgency program, South Vietnam had an excellent chance at winning the war against the communists who were allowed by the Paris Peace Accord to remain in South Vietnam.

I believe North Vietnam knew that to comply with the Paris Peace Accord was to allow South Vietnam to defeat the communist insurgency in South Vietnam. Once North Vietnam knew that they could break their treaty with the US without adverse consequences, they no longer found it necessary to pretend to be fighting an insurgency war, so they planned a large conventional invasion.

North Vietnam tested our new President, Ford, by attacking Phuoc Long in South Vietnam on January 6, 1975. Since the United States didn't retaliate, North Vietnam launched an invasion with twenty divisions into South Vietnam in early March 1975. Without the support of the United States, North Vietnam successfully destroyed the South Vietnamese army, and Saigon fell on April 30, 1975. By seizing and holding Saigon, North Vietnam also effectively ended the internal war. As Clausewitz stated, "In countries subject to domestic strife, the center of gravity is generally the capital."[5]

When it came to resolve, North Vietnam had a significant advantage over the United States. Unlike US leaders who had to answer to US citizens, North Vietnam leaders considered their soldiers' lives of little value, expendable. Because the communist government of North Vietnam controlled their media, they were able to hide their heavy losses in South Vietnam from their citizens. North Vietnam also had a large enough population that they could always replace the soldiers they had lost.

The United States believed the enemy's center of gravity was initially their troops, and later in the war, their supplies. Consequently, General Westmoreland implemented a strategy to attrite the enemy force until they no longer had the capability to continue fighting. Unfortunately, the tactics Westmoreland implemented to destroy the enemies troops also cost an unacceptable number of US casualties.

US military leaders thought that over time, North Vietnam would eventually say they had had enough. However, the longer the war lasted, the more obvious it became that time was not on our side. It was the will of American citizens rather than of North Vietnam citizens that was deteriorating. Time ran out on us.

Consequences of Flawed Tactics

I will provide evidence with examples that the United States could have won if we had employed tactics that kept US casualties at an extremely low and acceptable level, while still stopping the infiltration of the enemy and destroying their weapons, supplies, and troops in order to provide security to the South Vietnamese. A convincing argument will be made to support the position that with proper tactics, the US military could have protected and kept the resolve of US citizens strong enough to enforce the 1973 Paris Peace Accord.

When combat commander plan a military operation they have a number of Course of Actions (C/A) to choose from. After analyzing the pros and cons of each he selects the one that will achieve the objective with the least amount of friendly casualties. Unfortunately, this was not done by most US commanders in Vietnam.

Most military analysts believe South Vietnam was clearly winning the counterinsurgency war against the communist forces that were allowed to remain in South Vietnam by the Paris Peace Accord. If the United States had been able to convince North Vietnam that the US was committed to enforcing the Paris Peace Accord and to stopping any invasion of South Vietnam with their conventional forces, there would be a non-communist government in South Vietnam today.

General Westmoreland was replaced by General Creighton Abrams in 1968, and the large scale search and destroy operations that resulted in the majority of US casualties were replaced by *clear and hold* operations. Additionally, maintaining the security of people in hamlets and villages replaced attrition of enemy forces as a primary objective.[6]

Abrams was more focused on the enemy's supply of weapons, ammunition, and food rather than on body count; Abrams *believed the supply was the enemy's center of gravity.* Incursions into Cambodia by US and Army of the Republic of Vietnam (ARVN) forces and into Laos by ARVN forces to destroy enemy supplies proved to significantly damage the NVA/VC's ability to conduct large scale operations within South Vietnam.

By mid-1970, the number of NVA/VC remaining in South Vietnam was at a level low enough that the ARVN could almost handle the threat on their own, with US advisors, equipment, and air support. Consequently, President Nixon's Vietnamization program which required turning the war fighting over to the Vietnamese was in full swing. After the US's Cambodian incursion, US ground maneuver units remaining in Vietnam continued to improve security and pacification within South Vietnam to the point where the ARVN could manage the war on their own.

By 1971, the ARVN conducted most of the search and destroy type of mission, and the number of US combat troops remaining in Vietnam had been reduced significantly. As a result the US experienced a substantial reduction in American casualties. Unfortunately, heavy US casualties in the past had already weakened the US citizens' resolve to the point that America was not willing to take the actions required to enforce the Paris Peace Accord signed on January 27, 1973.

Certainly, North Vietnam would never have invaded South Vietnam with a conventional attack if they thought the US would return to enforce the Paris Peace Accord. For North Vietnam to attack with conventional troops, using tanks out in the open, would have been suicide against the superior airpower of the United States. With US air superiority, the United States would have completely destroyed North Vietnam's army.

I conclude that the United States failed to achieve a lasting victory in the Vietnam War, because we lost our resolve, and that we lost our resolve because we lost an unacceptable number of US soldiers. In the next chapter, I argue that poor tactics caused higher casualties than necessary.

CHAPTER 5

Flawed Military Tactics

*Since they hated knowledge and did not choose to fear the
Lord, since they would not accept my advice and spurned my
rebuke, they will eat the fruit of their ways and be filled with
the fruit of their schemes. For the waywardness of the simple
will kill them, and the complacency of fools will destroy them.*

Proverb 1:29-32[1]

The decision made by US civilian leadership to not use our
overwhelming combat power within the borders of North Vietnam to
destroy their military, made the Vietnam conflict extremely challenging
for General Westmoreland, and later, for General Abrams. Even with these
self-imposed limitations, I believe both generals had winnable plans at the
strategic level; however, at the tactical level, they were executed poorly.

Poor US tactics failed to protect America's center of gravity (our
resolve) and also failed to effectively destroy the enemy's center of gravity
(military). Thus, the enemy destroyed America's center of gravity before
America could destroy theirs.

Both General Westmoreland and General Abrams focused on the
security of the people in the hamlets and villages. However, during
Westmoreland's command, to keep the enemy from planning and
conducting offensive operations that would endanger the villages, the
US had to continually search for the enemy and attack him. By the time
Abrams took command, there were fewer large NVA/VC camps remaining

in South Vietnam. Consequently, Abrams focused on a concept he called *search and hold*, rather than on *search and destroy*. Although there were fewer large NVA/VC troop bases in South Vietnam, there were still enough to present a threat. Therefore, there remained a need to search them out. In reality American forces never did hold terrain in the jungles. Other than changing the name to hold rather than destroy, I did not see much difference between the two concepts.

Abrams and Westmoreland understood that it was necessary to go on the offensive and conduct search and destroy operations to win. However, the way they conducted these operations was wrong. The decision to use conventional infantry units to stumble through the jungle searching and closing with the enemy to destroy him proved to be extremely ineffective and costly. Any good infantry officer should have foreseen how difficult it would be to use conventional infantry to surprise, fix and destroy the VC/NVA in their familiar jungle environment.

Unfortunately, Westmoreland was commissioned an artillery officer and Abrams an armor officer; neither had experience as an infantry platoon leader or a company commander in a jungle environment. This is not to say that the overall commander of military forces in Vietnam needed to be an infantry officer with jungle fighting experience. It does, however, insinuate that if one does not have the experience, one must be wise enough to heed the advice of those that do. Proverbs 15:22 states, "Plans fail for lack of counsel, but with many advisers they succeed."[2]

To support the overall hypothesis of this book, that God denied the US top brass the wisdom to employ winning tactics, I present an account of one of the first large US battles conducted in Vietnam. The tragic result of this battle should have sent a clear message to our senior military leaders that the practice of conducting search and destroy operations with conventional infantry units needed to be changed. Instead, Westmoreland and Abrams seemed to have been blinded to this reality, and continued to use the same failed tactics over and over throughout the war.

On November 14, 1965, at 10:48 a.m., the 1st Battalion, 7th US Cavalry conducted a helicopter assault into Landing Zone (LZ) X-Ray in order to search for an NVA regiment of approximately 1,500 troops believed to be in the area. Rather than one NVA regiment, there were three NVA regiments scattered around the area. Helicopters landing US troops into an obvious Landing Zone (LZ) deep in NVA territory was exactly what the NVA wanted. Almost as soon as the first lift of helicopters arrived, the NVA began moving troops towards LZ X-Ray to kill the Americans. Ironically, 1/7 Cavalry Battalion Commander Lieutenant Colonel (LTC) Moore's order before boarding the helicopters was to "take your battalion in there and find and kill him."[3] LTC Moore did not need to find the enemy; the enemy found him and his battalion. Within minutes, Moore had lost the initiative to the NVA, and within three days and two nights, his 450-man under strength battalion suffered 79 Americans killed and 120 wounded.

Because most of the NVA killed in the battle at LZ X-Ray were by US airstrikes and artillery, there is no way of knowing exactly how many NVA were killed. American units generally claimed that the enemy lost ten times as many as the Americans. Consequently, reported figures were not always close to reality. However, the number of the enemy killed was also not all that important to the American population. They only paid attention to how many Americans were killed. American citizens knew exactly how many Americans had already been killed in the war and how many were killed in the current week, but they had no idea, nor did they even care, how many of the enemy had been killed. Attrition of the enemy was important, but some commanders failed to weigh the cost in American lives of attaining it.

On the afternoon of November 16, the 1/7 Cavalry was extracted from LZ X-Ray along with all their dead and wounded. However, the 2nd Battalion, 7th Cavalry, and 2nd Battalion, 5th Cavalry, who had both marched into LZ X-Ray on foot earlier in the fight to strengthen the 1/7 Cavalry defenses, remained at LZ X-Ray.

Because a B-52 airstrike was scheduled for the area, on November 17, the 2/7 Cavalry moved out of LZ X-Ray and marched to a clearing in the jungle two miles north, called LZ Albany. For the same reason, the 2/5 Cavalry marched two miles northeast to LZ Columbus, where two of the four artillery batteries that supported the operation were located.

Once the NVA saw that the 2/7 Cavalry was moving on foot in the direction of a clearing that could be used as a pickup zone or a night defensive position, they moved their fresh reserve battalion into position to ambush the 600-yard-long US infantry column. They initiated their ambush just short of LZ Albany on the afternoon of November 17, and the attack lasted through the night and into the early morning of November 18. The result was even worse than that at LZ X-Ray: the battalion suffered 155 Americans killed and 130 wounded.[4]

The NVA also attacked LZ Columbus, but the 2/5 Cavalry and artillery units were in prepared defensive positions with good fields of fire. They cranked down the twelve howitzer barrels and fired beehive rounds (thousands of small nail-shaped darts) directly into the enemy. The NVA attackers were driven off with heavy losses. This is a clear example of the benefit of fighting the enemy from an advantageous position.

Sadly, even though most heavy American casualties were the result of search and destroy operations similar to the one described above, this method of operation was never changed. How could intelligent generals like Westmoreland and Abrams not have seen the obvious reasons for the tragic results of the battles at LZ X-Ray and Albany? How could they not have changed their method of finding and destroying the NVA/VC in the jungles of Vietnam? My intent is not to convince the reader that searching for the enemy and killing him was unnecessary, but that there could have been a better way to do so that would have caused fewer US casualties.

I identify a concept that could have accomplished the search and destroy missions with fewer casualties. Throughout the Vietnam War, though, God did not provide our senior military leaders with the insight to see it.

During his time as the overall commander in Vietnam, General Westmoreland never did change how search and destroy operations were conducted. General Abrams finally realized that battalion-size units searching for the enemy in jungles that were familiar to the NVA/VC could not employ the element of surprise. However, he never fully understood just how difficult it was for US conventional troops to search and fight in this environment against the NVA/VC, regardless of unit size. Ultimately, neither Westmoreland nor Abrams ever discovered a better way of conducting search and destroy operations.

When General Abrams took overall command in Vietnam, he claimed to have devised new tactics. Abrams's new tactics called for getting out in smaller ground units to make contact with the enemy, and then moving unengaged units in to pile on the area. In the book *A Better War*, Abrams is quoted describing his concern over getting the ARVN to adjust to his new tactic: "The idea of going out in company strength, or platoon strength—whoo!—only battalions! That was the only way they wanted to go. Well a battalion—it's like trying to sneak up on the enemy with a tank, it's just too noisy. If you want to get him, if you want to find him, you've got to do it with these small outfits. And then, once you get him, then everybody jump in! Well, they've been working on it."[5]

Abrams knew correctly that US and ARVN battalion-size search and destroy operations always failed to surprise the enemy. Unfortunately, he incorrectly believed an infantry platoon or company was small enough to sneak up on the enemy. For example, if a platoon (35 men) or a company (150 men) landed in LZ X-Ray they would have been all killed. A better concept that I will discuss in the seventh chapter employs a small highly trained five-man reconnaissance patrol that is able to be inserted into the jungle undetected and to search the area undetected. Once the enemy is located the reconnaissance team does not engage the enemy, but rather marks the enemy's location and calls-in a B-52 airstrike. Since most of the enemy in the battle at LZ X-Ray were killed from airstrikes and artillery, the mission could have been achieve with a lot fewer American casualties.

First Tour Experience

My experience from my first tour as a leg infantry platoon leader taught me that even a platoon usually made too much noise when moving through the jungle to actually surprise the NVA/VC in their base camp. The enemy commander usually had a choice—either to immediately leave the area, or to set up an ambush. The US unit would either find an empty base camp full of booby traps or run into an enemy ambush.

During my first tour, I conducted numerous search and destroy operations and located many enemy base camps; all of them were empty of the enemy and full of booby traps. There was one exception, and that one had a few VC stay-behinds to set off Chinese Communist (CHICOM) claymore mines to kill any US troops searching their evacuated camp. To the infantryman, the CHICOM claymore mine was possibly the enemy's most devastating and feared weapon. Unlike a conventional land mine, the claymore is usually command-detonated and directional, meaning it is fired by remote-control and shoots a pattern of metal balls into the kill zone like grape shot fired out of a cannon (See figure 1).

I located the VC base camp mentioned above during my first tour, when I was searching a jungle with my infantry platoon. The VC base camp had a number of huts that appeared to have just been evacuated. I put out security and began searching the huts for documents, weapons, and equipment when I heard one of the men that I had on security yell: "Claymore!" I hit the ground. My security man, who had yelled the warning, tried to run, and when the claymore detonated, he was hit and fell to the ground. The claymore was command-detonated by a VC hiding in a spider hole (a small tunnel with a camouflaged trap door). I immediately went to where my man went down. As I looked up, I saw another claymore facing in our direction. Because a CHICOM claymore is attached to the top of a tripod, I was able to shoot it over with my M-16. I then attempted to provide aid to my man—unfortunately, he was already dead. I retrieved him and pulled my platoon out of the camp. I called in airstrikes and artillery on the camp, moved back in and continued the search without further incident. I didn't realize how close I came to dying that day until my Vietnamese scout dog-handler went into his rucksack for a dog food can. When the claymore detonated, the dog handler was behind me. We both hit the ground and I saw leaves falling down on me. I hadn't known just how close the projectiles were until I saw the holes in the dog food cans that were in the dog-handler's rucksack.

Another time, in 1966, while searching an enemy base camp along with the entire company, I saw a sergeant from another platoon about to pull a wire that ran across a tunnel entrance. He was about to do so with his bare hands, rather than using a grappling hook and rope. I yelled, "Don't pull that wire!" To this day, I don't know why, but he pulled it—there was an enormous explosion. The sergeant literally disintegrated.

During my first tour, I also experienced the consequences of an enemy commander opting to conduct an ambush against a US unit searching through the jungle for his camp. In 1966, our entire infantry battalion conducted an air assault into a dried-up lake deep in the jungle, and set up a Night Defensive Position (NDP). Each day over the next week, the three line companies would conduct company-size search and destroy operations using the cloverleaf technique from the battalion NDP. My company commander rotated the lead platoon each day when conducting these movements. On this particular day, my platoon was the rear platoon in the file. We had traveled approximately two kilometers into the jungle when I noticed that the underbrush was turned down and tied to create an area of *tangle foot*. Except for my platoon, the entire company had already moved into the area. I knew the underbrush didn't grow this way. I had just asked my radio operator for the handset in order to tell the company commander that they had walked into the kill zone of an ambush, when the enemy initiated their attack.

The enemy conducting the ambush stayed hidden in camouflaged spider holes, and set off command-detonated claymores and other types of explosives. Because we couldn't see the enemy, we fired out to our flanks and walked artillery in on both sides of our file as close as we could. The company ended up with eighteen casualties before the NVA pulled back. Because my platoon was not in the kill zone, we hadn't suffered any casualties, and we provided front, flank, and rear security for the company while also cutting an ankle-high trail out of the jungle so that the wounded and dead could be carried out on field expedient poncho stretchers. As we moved back, enemy snipers fired into the battalion perimeter, hoping that our battalion would fire in our direction as we returned. I had good radio communication with the battalion, though, so their trick didn't work.

I conducted a head-count as the company came out of the jungle back into our night defensive position. A man from one of the other platoons passed by, smiling but smelling terrible. I asked what he was smiling for and he said that when he hit the ground during the ambush, he looked up and saw a CHICOM claymore staring him in the face. All of a sudden he heard a pop—the claymore's electric blasting cap went off, but it didn't detonate the claymore. The man literally defecated in his pants, but he was a happy and very lucky soldier.

Evidence of Senior Leaders' Lack of Knowledge

General Abrams's so called new "Piling On" tactic of sending out a small unit to find the enemy or as bait, and then once contact is made, everybody should jump in, had major flaws. Piling on in a jungle battle, in the enemy's territory, can have disastrous results. It usually only provides the enemy more targets to shoot at. Although "massing your force at a specific location to overwhelm the opponent" is one of the Principles of War, with the devastating lethality of today's weapon systems, massing dismounted troops is a bad idea when attacking a guerrilla force in the jungle. The principle of massing is still valid, but, massing firepower rather than troops usually makes for a better outcome.

Even for General Abrams's clear and hold strategy, some commanders failed to understand the danger of the jungle. The battle of the 101st Airborne Division's 3rd Brigades on May 10, 1969, up Hill 937 (known as "Hamburger Hill" because troops felt they were attacking into a meat grinder), resulted in 47 US killed in action (KIA) and 308 wounded in action (WIA). Most of the 691 enemy dead found on the battlefield were killed by artillery, tactical air, helicopter gunships, and B-52 bombers.[6] I do not know of any battle against the NVA/VC in an enemy jungle base area in which the US infantry was able to surround the enemy and fix them in place so they could be destroyed with direct or indirect fire. The NVA and VC were not stupid. They always had the flexibility to slip away from American troops unfamiliar with their defenses and tunnel systems located deep within the heavy jungle.

It was no secret that some generals and colonels were willing to send infantry companies or platoons into the jungle as bait. They hoped the unit would be ambushed so they could pile on additional troops in order to obtain a large enemy body count. In his 1989 book *Mud Soldiers: Life inside the new American Army*, George C. Wilson quotes a conversation between First Infantry Division Commander General DePuy and Lieutenant Libs immediately after the two-day battle of Xa Cam My April 11 to April 12, 1966). The 134 men of Charlie Company, 2nd Battalion, 16th Infantry, First Infantry Division were ambushed by the Viet Cong while conducting a search and destroy operation approximately 42 miles northwest of Saigon. They suffered 35 killed and 72 wounded. Libs is quoted as saying to General DePuy, "You put us out there as bait." General DePuy said he wanted to know exactly what happened, so Libs went through every phase of the battle. The lieutenant ended his briefing by saying, "You walked us into a holocaust, General." The General replied, "Yeah, but there's no other way to get a fight going." The after-action report of the battle estimated 150 Vietcong were killed and driven off the battlefield.[7] *The question, therefore, is not whether the objective was important or whether the mission was accomplished, but whether it could have been achieved with fewer US casualties.*

There are many ways to accomplish a mission, but there is only one best way. At the operational level of planning, a commander should develop a *commander's estimate*. This requires considering all courses of action (C/A) that are possible to accomplish the mission, listing all the advantages and disadvantages of each C/A, and then determining which C/A provides the *best* results. In the Vietnam Conflict, the best C/A was usually the one that eliminated the threat/enemy and resulted in the fewest US casualties. C/As that worked in the past should always be considered and evaluated; however, the more diverse and out-of-the-box C/As considered, the better the results of the final decision.

Throughout the war, US commanders in Vietnam continually selected the same costly C/A to find and kill the enemy. The C/A used over and over was to insert an infantry platoon, company, or battalion by helicopter into a dried-up lake or other obvious Landing Zone, and then search the jungle for enemy base camps. This repetition established a pattern and lost us the element of surprise. Consequently, the NVA/VC were able to anticipate US actions, and gain the initiative.

Sun Tzu's *The Art of War*, written twenty-five hundred years ago, is the earliest existing book of strategy. It warns commanders not to use the same tactic over and over again. Sun Tzu says, "Everyone may know the control through which we are able to achieve victory, but cannot know the control through which we are able to determine victory. So, our victories in battles will not be repeated and our responsive control will be unlimited."[8]

First Tour Experience

I personally met General DePuy once while I was in Vietnam. That was approximately seven months after the battle of Xa Cam My. In October 1966, I had a tank platoon attached to my leg infantry platoon. We were given the mission of conducting a search and destroy operation in a jungle area close to the 3rd Brigade, First Infantry Division's headquarters in Lai Khe, not far from where the battle of Xa Cam My took place. I was about to bust into the jungle with my five attached tanks positioned in a

V-formation and my infantry platoon deployed behind the tanks, when General DePuy's helicopter landed behind us. He asked what we were doing and I told him that a recon aircraft had detected an ox-cart going into the jungle area the night before, and we were tasked to see what we could find. DePuy said that a US unit had run into a large VC unit a number of months ago and took heavy casualties, so if we ran into any enemy we should back off and call in air and artillery. I said we would and he took off again in his helicopter.

It turned out that we found a large VC base camp, but it was empty. If there had been any enemies in the base, they had probably heard the roar of the tanks and the sound of trees falling and decided to run. I had the tanks run through the camp a few times to destroy it and then we pulled back out of the jungle. As long as the terrain was not too marshy or mountainous, the combined armor and infantry team proved to be extremely effective. Tanks could knock down trees and brush and set off booby traps and mines. The infantry provided the tanks flank and rear security as we moved through the jungle. Although a combined infantry and armor force will never surprise the enemy in his base camp, it is a very difficult unit to successfully ambush in the jungle. Unfortunately, following tanks as they moved through the jungle was like climbing over a brush pile all day long. I went through three radio operators (RTO) while on this particular operation.

General Depuy's directive for me to pull my force back and call in air and artillery leads me to believe the General had changed his view on how to deal with the enemy after the battle of Xa Cam My. I believe that, overall, General Depuy was a good division commander, and the First Infantry Division was one of the finest divisions in Vietnam. In all fairness, some of Lieutenant Libs' men were killed by friendly artillery fire during the battle of Xa Cam My. General DePuy could not be blamed for the US casualties that were caused by the artillery unit's mistake.

General Depuy was right about needing to get the enemy to fight. Almost all contact with the NVA/VC during the Vietnam Conflict was enemy initiated; using bait was a way to engage them. However, putting the bait in the jungle where the enemy had the advantage was a bad idea. On the other hand, using some form of bait to draw the enemy into a vulnerable situation is wise as long as it doesn't actually put friendly troops into a vulnerable position. The enemy can be tricked into thinking the friendly troops are vulnerable; in reality, they should actually be in an advantageous position. I describe such an operation later in the book, at the beginning of the Katum chapter, when the construction of a US Special Forces camp was used as bait.

Sun Tzu writes, "To weaken the enemy exercise unconventional means. Through enticement with advantages, show gains to lure them."[9] Tricking the enemy into doing something that will put him at a disadvantage is a major part of warfare. Even at platoon level during my first tour, we were always looking for ways to trick the enemy into making deadly mistakes. For example, in 1966, I placed-three man listening posts (LP) out around our night defensive position each night. Because our mission at the time was the pacification of a particular Vietnamese village, our NDP was semi-permanent. Consequently, the VC would target our LPs at night. One of the three men I lost during my first tour was killed after a VC located one of our LPs and threw a grenade at it. To counter the enemy's assault on our LPs, I had my men set out two LP decoys. They dug two foxholes and placed three manikin dummies in the bottom of each. The plan was to go out to the decoy positions as soon as it became dark, set up the dummies, then low crawl to an ambush position and wait for the VC.

As soon as it was dark, the two LPs left the NDP perimeter. As one of the LPs approached its decoy site one of the men using his starlight scope saw a VC crouched down behind some bushes, and rather than immediately shooting the VC he yelled, "I see VC!" Unfortunately, the VC immediately threw a hand grenade and it severely injured my man's leg. It was common for a VC traveling in areas where he might have contact to hold a US grenade in his hand with the pin already pulled so that he could immediately throw it and break contact. If he didn't have contact and was no longer in a dangerous area, he would bend the end of the grenade handle-up and put a rubber band around the grenade to hold the handle down.

The other LP that went out successfully set up their decoy LP as planned and moved to their ambush site, which happened to be in a Vietnamese cemetery. At approximately 0200 hours, a VC threw a grenade into the decoy LP, and as he attempted to run away, one of my men popped up from behind a grave and killed the VC with his shotgun.

The next morning, we searched the area where the first VC was sighted, and found a CHICOM claymore mine (See figure 1). The wire had not yet been rolled out. If the LP had not seen the VC while going to their decoy, they may have been able to successfully move to their ambush site and ambush the VC. On the other hand, if the LP hadn't seen the VC and hadn't been required to set up a decoy LP, but rather move into a real LP, the claymore surely would have killed all three men.

Failure to Change Tactics

The point to be made in studying these examples is that tricking the enemy by using bait is good; however, using a vulnerable leg infantry unit in the jungle as bait usually proved disastrous. Conventional mechanized or leg infantry units seldom surprised the VC/NVA in the jungle, and when contact was made, most of the enemy casualties were not the result of small arms fire from the infantry force, but rather from airstrikes and artillery.

Neither Westmoreland nor Abrams understood this. According to David Maraniss in his book *They Marched into the Sunlight*, Westmoreland would ask the First Infantry Division commander General Hays why his troops did not pursue the enemy at the end of the battle and instead allowed them to slip away. Hays is quoted as telling Westmoreland, "we pursued by fire [artillery and air] and that risk to troops pursuing overland into the territory more familiar to the Viet Cong was not worth it unless we knew where they were."[10]

Both Westmoreland and Abrams underestimated the capability of the enemy and the advantage they had when fighting in familiar jungle. They put pressure on their subordinates to be more aggressive against the enemy in the jungle. What these two generals did not understand was that when fighting in the jungle, no matter how aggressive US ground forces were, they could never outmaneuver the NVA/VC in their own familiar terrain.

Although official military reports on battles resulting from search and destroy operations claim victory over the VC/NVA, most lacked the element of surprise and were enemy-initiated. US troops suffered large numbers of casualties in the initial phases of the battles. *They Marched into the Sunlight* provides an understanding of how most search and destroy operation's battles were initiated in Vietnam. Maraniss includes an interview taken after the war with General Vo Minh Triet. Triet was a Lieutenant Colonel and the commander of the Viet Cong's First Regiment, which battled the 2nd Battalion, 28th Infantry of the First Infantry Division at Long Nguyen Secret Zone, 12.3 miles north of Lai Khe during Operation Shenandoah II.

On October 17, 1967, the 2/28 Infantry conducted a battalion-size search and destroy operation in the Long Nguyen Secret Zone. Shortly after entering the jungle from their NDP, they saw fresh tracks and enemy troops further in the jungle, and immediately pursued them. Within minutes they started to receive a heavy volume of fire from both the trees and bunkers in the ground. After a two hour battle 58 US soldiers were dead and 31 wounded. Surprisingly, Westmoreland called the battle a meeting engagement and a success, rather than an enemy ambush and US defeat. Although only a few enemy bodies were found, the official report claimed 103 VC were killed. [11]

In Triet's interview, he said the Americans were kept under observation as soon as they moved into the area. He said, "The fresh tracks along the trail, the sighting of enemy soldiers in the distance – these were lures designed to draw the Americans deeper into a trap." Triet already had two of his battalions in position in the west and a third moving into position from the east. When the American soldiers were just where Triet wanted them, which was in front of his camouflaged bunkers, machine guns, and preset claymores – he gave the signal to fire. [12]

This chapter claims that because of flawed tactics used to conduct search and destroy operations, the US suffered a larger number of casualties than necessary. The following chapter provides evidence to support this claim and verify that the tragic scenario described in the preceding paragraph was played out over and over throughout the war.

CHAPTER 6

Search and Destroy Operations

To provide the reader with a clearer understanding of how ineffective search and destroy operations were, and of the failure of senior leaders to change their flawed tactics, I have included examples of numerous US search and destroy operations conducted, ranging from one of the first operations in Vietnam to one of the last. My intent is not to convince the reader that searching for the enemy and killing him was unnecessary, but rather that there could have been a better way to do so that might have resulted in fewer US casualties.

Not all failed search and destroy operations that took place in Vietnam are presented below, but I have included enough of them to show that failed operations were not restricted to the Army, the Marines, a specific division, or a specific regiment.

Because US commanders did not change their search and destroy tactics, the tragic scenarios of most failed search and destroy operations are very similar. To avoid redundancy, I refer the reader to the detailed information provided in the previous chapter on the November, 1965, LZ X-Ray/LZ Albany operation[1] and the October, 1967, Long Nguyen Secret Zone operation.[2]

On November 14-16, 1965, the 450-man 1st Battalion, 7th US Cavalry suffered 79 Americans killed and 120 wounded during a search and destroy operation in the Ia Drang.[3]

On November 17–18, 1965, the 2nd Battalion, 7th U.S. Cavalry was ambushed moving to their pickup zone (PZ), LZ Albany, and suffered 155 Americans killed and 130 wounded.[4]

On April 11, 1966, the 134-man Charlie Company, 2nd Battalion, 16th Infantry, First Infantry Division conducted a search and destroy operation near Xa Cam My, 42 miles northwest of Saigon. The company ran into a VC ambush and suffered 35 killed and 72 wounded. The after-action report of the battle estimated 150 VC were killed.[5]

On April 24-May 5, 1967, two battalions of the 3rd Marine Regiment lost 160 men and 746 were wounded in a twelve-day battle to drive NVA troops off three hills near Khe Sanh in Quangtin Province.[6]

On May 9, 1967, a 3rd Marine Regiment unit was attacked by the NVA nine miles northwest of Khe Sanh. In the five-hour battle, the US Marines suffered 24 casualties.[7]

On May 18–31, 1967, the 26th Marines conducted Operation Prairie IV east of Khe Sanh to clear the DMZ. Two fortified hills occupied by the NVA were stormed by the Marines and captured. The operation resulted in 164 Marines killed and 999 wounded.[8]

On June 2, 1967, a US 5th Marine battalion was ambushed in the Hiepdus Valley by a 2900-man NVA regiment. The Marines report killing 540; however, they suffered 73 dead and 139 wounded.[9]

On June 12–17 1967, the US First Infantry Division conducted a drive into the jungles of War Zone D, 50 miles north of Saigon, in an attempt to trap three VC battalions. The First Infantry Division claimed to have killed at least 150 VC during the five-day operation. Unfortunately, the VC ambushed one of the US units while they were moving to their PZ. The ambush cost the Americans 31 dead and 113 wounded.[10]

On June 22, 1967, a 130-man infantry company of the 173rd US Airborne Brigade was ambushed by the NVA near Dakto 28 miles northeast of Saigon. 88 Americans were killed and 34 wounded. Only 106 NVA were reported killed.[11]

On July 2, 1967, a platoon of the 9th Marine Regiment was ambushed by 500 NVA just south of the DMZ, and 35 Marines were killed. Marine reinforcements were rushed in. After intense fighting, Marine casualties totaled 96 killed and 211 wounded.[12]

On July 2, 1967, two companies of the 9th Marine Regiment were attacked by the NVA and suffered heavy losses. Four battalions were helicoptered into the area to reinforce the two companies and maneuver against the flank of the enemy. On July 14, the NVA slipped away after losing an estimated 1301. The US losses were 159 dead and 45 wounded.[13]

On July 10, 1967, while conducting a sweep of the Dakto area near Kontum, a 173rd Airborne Brigade battalion was ambushed by the NVA. The American losses were 26 killed and 49 wounded.[14]

On July 11, 1967, while conducting a search and destroy operation, a US 4th Infantry Division unit was ambushed five miles south of Ducco in the Central Highlands. American losses were 35 killed and 31 wounded.[15]

On September 4–7, 1967, units of the US 5th Marine Regiment fought the NVA in the Queson Valley, 25 miles south of Danang. During the battle, 114 Americans were killed and 376 NVA died.[16]

On October 17, 1967, the 2/28 Infantry of the 1st Infantry Division was ambushed while conducting Ong Thanh search and destroy operation north of Lai Khe. The US suffered 58 killed and 31 wounded. The details of this tragedy are presented in the fifth chapter of this book.[17]

On November 19–22, 1967, the 173rd Airborne Brigade attacked Hill 875, while defended by NVA occupying dug-in positions. The NVA eventually abandoned their positions, but not until the Brigade suffered 158 men killed. The attack on Hill 875 was part of a larger battle that started on November 3 when approximately 4000 US troops from the 4th Division and the 173rd Airborne Brigade fought about 6000 NVA troops in the Central Highlands around Dakto. During the nineteen-day battle, an estimated 1455 NVA were killed while 285 US troops were killed, 985 were wounded, and 18 went missing. Westmoreland briefed officials at the Pentagon on November 22, 1967 and said that the battle was "the beginning of a great defeat for the enemy."[18]

On March 2, 1968, US troops were ambushed four miles north of Tansonnhut Air Base while conducting a search and destroy operation. The US suffered 48 men killed and 28 wounded.[19]

On May 10, 1969, the 101st Airborne Division's 3rd Brigade, while searching the jungles of the Ashua valley, found the NVA entrenched on Apbia Mountain (Hill 937). After 11 infantry assaults, air strikes, and artillery fire the stronghold was captured. The 11 infantry assaults up the hill resulted in the US suffering 47 killed and 308 wounded. Most of the 691 enemy dead found on the battlefield were killed by artillery, tactical air, helicopter gunships, and B-52 bombers.[20]

On August 17–26, 1969, 1200 US Americal Division and ARVN troops ran into a well-defended NVA complex of tunnels and bunkers. The result was 60 Americans killed and an estimated 650 NVA killed. During the battle on August 24, the men of Alpha Company of the 196th Light Infantry Brigade refused an order from their commander to continue combat operations to reach a downed helicopter. The company had attempted to reach the helicopter during the previous five days and received heavy losses. The battalion commander sent his executive officer to the field to give the men a pep talk. The men fought their way to the helicopter the following day; however, all eight men were dead.[21]

On October 24, 1969, a US 25th Infantry Division unit of 200 troops ran into a NVA/VC unit 28 miles north of Saigon. American losses were 10 killed and 12 wounded while enemy losses were estimated at 47.[22]

On February 13, 1970, US Marines were ambushed in the Queson valley. Marine losses were 13 killed and 12 wounded while 6 enemy were killed.[23]

On February 14, 1970, eight US soldiers were killed and 30 wounded in a NVA ambush near the Cambodian border. NVA losses were estimated to be 31 killed.[24]

As evidenced from the tragic results of the above examples, using conventional leg infantry units to conduct search and destroy operations resulted in large numbers of US casualties. The fact that almost all of the enemy casualties suffered in the above battles were the result of US artillery and air strikes, rather than infantry light weapons, makes the heavy loss of US infantry troops even more tragic.

I believe all would agree, after an honest review of the battles that took place in Vietnam, that the tactic of using conventional infantry units to find the enemy in the jungle and destroy him was seriously flawed. It should be noted that because most of the above battles were enemy initiated, most of the American casualties happened within a few hours, and in some cases minutes. Clearly this tactic caused extremely high numbers of American casualties; obviously, it was wrong. The fact that America's senior leaders did not see this obvious mistake and change their tactics supports my position that God denied them wisdom.

The next chapter does not suggest that search and destroy operations should not have been conducted; rather it identifies better tactics that should have been used to conduct them.

CHAPTER 7

Better Search and Destroy Tactics

*The general who can assess the value of ground maneuvers
his enemy into dangerous terrain and keeps clear of it himself.
He chooses the ground on which he wishes to engage, draws
his enemy to it, and there gives battle.*

Sun Tzu[1]

In light of the ineffective and disastrous results of conducting the search
and destroy operations with conventional infantry units, it would have
been better to have infiltrated quiet five-man Long Range Reconnaissance
Patrols (LRRP) to search for enemy base camps. If the LRRP found an
enemy base camp, they could call in a B-52 airstrike.

If B-52 strikes were no-notice surprise attacks as in Cambodia, they
were extremely effective. When we searched base areas in Cambodia after
B-52 strikes, most of the NVA were dead and those not dead were in no
condition to fight.

Attached to my infantry company I had ten former NVA and VC who
had changed sides to work for the United States military called Kit Carson
Scouts. Some of them were excellent and others were similar to Gomer
Pyle. When I asked them if they were afraid of B-52 strikes they told me
because of a requirement to notify the Vietnamese province chief three
days prior to a strike, the NVA/VC never feared a B-52 strike in South
Vietnam. They always received a three-day warning from their spies and
were able to move out of the area.

In addition to poor operational security (OPSEC), B-52s remained under the control of the Strategic Air Command (SAC) and were not responsive to the ground commanders in Vietnam.

Current examples of the effectiveness of B-52 strikes when responsive to the ground commander are the B-52 strikes in the early stages of the 2001 Afghanistan War. With only 300 US Army Special Forces and a few CIA men on the ground traveling in small teams with the Northern Alliance units, the Taliban was driven out of power in Afghanistan. The United States was able to accomplish this because they had B-52s continually circling above Afghanistan and ready to immediately respond to the Special Forces team on the ground. The B-52s could either drop a 2000-pound GPS-guided bomb onto a specific point target or carpet-bomb an entire ridge line with 500- and 750-pound dumb bombs when the Northern Alliance needed them. When the enemy was not given a three-day warning, B-52 strikes proved highly effective.

Since OPSEC was a major problem in Vietnam, *restricted areas* needed to be assigned to LRRPs for extended periods of time, and B-52s had to be kept on standby to immediately respond to any LRRP's find. Using B-52 strikes in restricted areas would have eliminated the requirement of notifying the Vietnamese ahead of time.

In Vietnam, LRRPs emplaced beacons to direct the aircraft to the targets. The beacons provided the pilots with a relatively accurate method of finding the enemy in jungle-covered terrain. Today, however, with new GPS technology and improved smart bombs, using LRRPs to locate the enemy and keeping B-52 bombers on standby would prove to be even more effective.

Because of the importance of establishing restricted areas in a counterinsurgency, a further definition is provided. A restricted area is not to be confused with a *free-fire zone*. A restricted area is one where all personnel are restricted from entering unless they receive approval from the headquarters that designated the area. No one can enter or fire into the designated restricted area unless the commander assigned the restricted Area of Operation (AO) is notified.[2]

The restricted area control measure, therefore, allows the assigned commander to employ tactics and weapon systems without the fear of killing or injuring civilians or friendly troops. For civilians' own protection, establishing control measures such as restricted areas and curfews is critical in counterinsurgencies. Civilians must be informed that in this type of warfare, some of their freedom of movement will be restricted until the war is over.

Unlike a restricted area, a free-fire zone does not restrict the movement of civilians and other friendly forces within its area. Therefore, one cannot assume that anyone found in a free-fire zone is an enemy. In Vietnam, this meant that a soldier was authorized to fire at any person who could be identified as an enemy soldier without receiving permission from a higher headquarters.[3] Therefore, the distinction between a restricted area and a free-fire zone is huge. While commanding a Navy fast boat, former Secretary of State John Kerry ordered his crew to fire at a *sampan* on a river in Vietnam; an unarmed man and child were killed. Contrary to Kerry's justification that they were in a free-fire zone, the shooting of any individual who *is not* carrying an enemy weapon, wearing an enemy uniform or clearly identified in another way as an enemy soldier within a free-fire zone is a crime.[4]

This commentary on the usefulness of LRRPs in searching for the enemy is not meant to suggest there is no use for conventional leg infantry units. Because conventional leg infantry units can either quickly airmobile into position or quietly walk into position without being detected at night, the following missions were very effective and resulted in light casualties:

1. Hammer and Anvil: use leg infantry as a blocking force and mechanized and armor teams as the pushing force.
2. Providing the cordon around villages while ARVN troops search the village for enemy troops and supplies.
3. Conducting day and night ambushes.
4. Providing a quick reaction force when the enemy is in a vulnerable position or friendly forces need reinforcement.

Additionally, leg infantry units are necessary in operations such as airbase, firebase, and supply depot security, as well as urban warfare (fighting in cities). However, searching the jungle for the enemy in hopes of finding him and destroying him can be better accomplished with LRRPs and on-call B-52s.

If it was required for conventional troops to enter the jungle, and the terrain was not mountainous or marshy, a combined mechanized infantry and armored team or task force tended to be more effective than a leg infantry unit. A mechanized infantry unit with tanks attached could bust through the jungle to locate the enemy base camps. Although the enemy troops would be gone, the US unit could destroy the enemy's supplies and camp. Enemy booby traps were not effective against armor and the enemy was normally smart enough not to engage a mechanized infantry unit, knowing about the heavy firepower that they could deliver. The enemy usually returned once the US units pulled out of their base camp. *Mechanical ambushes* (MA) could be left behind to kill some of the enemy and demoralize many more. (Mechanical ambushes will be explained in chapter 11.)

These tactics address the use of US conventional maneuver units. However, if the host nation had maneuver units such as armor and infantry units, then it would be wise to provide each of their battalion-size maneuver units with a US liaison/coordination team of approximately six men, and use them in place of a US maneuver unit. The US liaison team would be able to call in US artillery, close air, lift helicopter, and resupply support. In other words, US ground combat maneuver units are a last resort. This policy would provide US airpower and supplies to an ally force that lacked it, while keeping US ground forces in reserve in a well defendable position. It would produce fewer US casualties, thereby protecting the United States' center of gravity.

How could two intelligent commanders like Westmoreland and Abrams not have seen that their tactics were allowing the enemy to successfully attack the United States' center of gravity? The manner in which search and destroy operations were conducted was not only flawed, it was too predictable; the enemy took advantage of this. Leaders in combat should be, as SunTzu says, "as unpredictable as rain clouds, striking like thunder and lightning."[5]

CHAPTER 8

Consequences of America's Lost Resolve

We tested Ford's resolve by attacking Phuoc Long. When Ford kept American B-52s in their hangers, our leadership decided on a big offensive against South Vietnam

North Vietnam's Bui Tin[1]

When US ground combat troops departed Vietnam, the ARVN did relatively well at fighting the counter guerrilla war, as long as the US was still providing advisors and air support. The ARVN even countered NVA larger conventional attacks that used tanks and armored vehicles.

As long as North Vietnam complied with the January 1973 Paris Peace Accord, the ARVN seemed able to hold their own against the communist forces, even after the US withdrew all their combat forces. By many accounts the South Vietnamese were winning the counterinsurgency war in South Vietnam against the communist forces that were authorized to remain in South Vietnam by the Paris Peace Accord. However, when Nixon resigned, the North Vietnamese believed they could break the treaty with the US without any adverse consequences, and gain a chance of winning the war in South Vietnam.

In early December, 1974, North Vietnam tested the United States' commitment to South Vietnam by breaking the Paris Peace Accord. They sent conventional forces from North Vietnam into South Vietnam and attacked Phuoc Long. Because the United States refused to come to South Vietnam's assistance, on January 6, 1975, Phuoc Long Province fell to the enemy.

Unfortunately, the United States' failure to respond to North Vietnam's blatant disregard for the Paris Peace Accord and their attack on Phuoc Long, North Vietnam rightly believed that the US would not retaliate against them, even with B-52s, if North Vietnam conducted an all-out invasion. Consequently, in early March, 1975, North Vietnam conducted a massive conventional attack into South Vietnam, and Saigon fell.

The United States lost an enormous amount of credibility and status in the world when we failed to enforce the Paris Peace Accord. This emboldened tyrants such as Saddam Hussein and convinced them that the United States lacked the willingness to stop their aggression.

I believe the US's goals in Vietnam were honorable; however, our failure to take any action against North Vietnam when they broke the treaty was shameful. Those who actively spread the communists' false propaganda and bamboozled Congress and the American people about US efforts in Indochina share much of the responsibility for the blood and the enormous scale of suffering inflicted by the communists not only in Vietnam, but in Cambodia and Laos as well.

False information about Vietnam, however, was not the only or primary contributing factor to America's defeat. Much of this book is based on the hypothesis that flawed tactics were used during most of the Vietnam conflict, and that better tactics would have prevented the United States' defeat. I define better tactics as tactics that accomplish a mission more effectively and with fewer US casualties. Since the number of US casualties had a major impact on America's lack of resolve or willingness to enforce the Paris Peace Accord, US senior leaders' failure to employ tactics that would have significantly reduced US casualties, was the overriding cause of America's final defeat in Vietnam.

As an infantry officer who served in Vietnam in 1966–67 and then again in 1970–71, it was obvious to me that the communists were being defeated in South Vietnam. Unfortunately, as I've mentioned, the misinformation spread by the media and naive peace demonstrators, the failure of the government to mobilize the public, and an unacceptable number of

American casualties significantly affected US citizens' willingness to stay in the fight.

Interestingly, we won a victory in January, 1973, but because US citizens' resolve was at such a low level after ten years of fighting, Congress was not willing to resume combat operations in order to enforce the hard won Paris Peace Accord. North Vietnam was allowed to break a treaty with the most powerful nation in the world, and lasting victory was not achieved. In his book *The Real War,* President Nixon correctly stated, "We won a victory after a long hard struggle, but then threw it away."[2]

Certainly, the North Vietnamese knew that the United States had overwhelming combat power to enforce the Paris Peace Accord. However, the American citizens' resolve was the United States' Achilles heel and North Vietnam rightly assumed that we no longer had the will to use our military power.

CHAPTER 9

Part I Reflections

If my people, who are called by my name, will humble themselves and pray and seek my face and turn from their wicked ways, then will I hear from heaven and will forgive their sin and will heal their land.

2 Chronicles 7:14[1]

The chapters of this book are extremely valuable and informative to those who want to know the truth about the combat in Vietnam. However, its main purpose is not to teach military tactics, but rather to be a confirmation of biblical truth. God loves us and for our own good He disciplines us when we disobey. Victory in war truly does rest with the Lord; therefore, if we as a nation expect success, we must pay attention to 2 Chronicles 7:14, quoted above, and not ignore God's correction.

This book provides support for the position that the Vietnam War would have been won if the correct tactics had been employed by the United States. The Bible tells us that it is God who provides men with the wisdom to win in battle, and this book provides clear evidence that God denied America's senior commanders the wisdom to employ sound tactics in Vietnam. It not only explains how these failed tactics contributed to the United States' defeat, but it identifies better tactics which, if used, could have led to victory.

Part I identified that the failed tactic that had the greatest negative impact on the final outcome of the Vietnam War was the tactic used to conduct search and destroy operations. The astonishing failure of the senior military leaders to see the futility of the tactic was the result of God denying them the wisdom to understand the problems of fighting in the jungles of Vietnam. A short review of the analysis to support this position is provided below:

Search and Destroy operations in the Vietnam War should not have been conducted using 30 – 200 man conventional leg infantry units. Rather, they should have been conducted by small five-men Long Range Surveillance Detachments to locate the enemy and mark targets for immediate B-52 airstrikes.

Chapter seven provides examples of heavy US casualties resulting from using conventional leg infantry units to conduct search and destroy operations in the jungles of Vietnam. These examples are evidence that these operations were flawed.

The high number of casualties sustained by conventional infantry units while in contact with the enemy in their own jungle environment, and the fact that these relatively large US units had to be extracted out of the contested area prior to being able to employ the most effective weapon system against the NVA/VC in the jungle, which was a B-52 strike, should have been reason enough not to use conventional infantry units to search for the enemy in this type of environment in the first place.

Part I suggests that Long Range Surveillance Detachments would have been a better element to conduct the search and destroy operations. However, for those operations to have been effective, a number of high level command and control changes would have been needed. The primary change required would be for the Strategic Air Command (SAC) commander to chop operational control (OPCON) of a portion of the B-52 force to the commander in Vietnam. Secondly, to ensure OPSEC and immediate responsiveness of B-52 firepower to the patrol on the ground, Long Range Surveillance Detachments would need to be assigned designated restricted areas in which to operate, and B-52 bombers would need to be on standby in order to respond to the discovery of a large concentration of enemy troops.

When I was Chief of Operations for Special Operations Command, Pacific, I was tasked with helping the United States Special Operations Command prepare the *Joint Special Operations Force Readiness Study* that was presented to the Joint Chiefs of Staff on April 6, 1988. One of my major contributions to the study was the concept of using Special Forces Operational Detachments to coordinate US airpower for foreign maneuver units that lacked their own. In 2001, during the invasion of Afghanistan, Special Forces teams linked up with the Northern Alliance and coordinated US airpower. The success of their mission demonstrated the effectiveness of B-52s when they are available to provide direct support to the ground commander.

Many commanders set a pattern when they conducted search and destroy operations in Vietnam. They inserted troops into obvious LZs and commenced to search the surrounding jungle for the enemy base camp. The enemy capitalized on their mistake by either setting up an ambush or an empty camp full of booby-traps for the Americans.

Clearly, using the same concept over and over failed to follow the *surprise* Principle of War, or, as Sun Tzu states, "All warfare is based on deception. A skilled general must be master of the complementary art of simulation; while creating shapes to confuse and delude the enemy he conceals his true dispositions and ultimate intent."[2]

Although the helicopter was used in the Korean War, it was not used to move large combat troops around the battlefield until Vietnam. The helicopter was a wonderful way to maneuver troops around Vietnam. Unfortunately, because commanders underestimated the enemy's ability to adjust to our use of the helicopter, the US failed to change the way it inserted troops into battle. The helicopter became, in many cases, a means by which targets were brought deep into the jungle for the VC/NVA to easily engage and thereby destroy the United States' center of gravity.

I believe many commanders were overly anxious to engage the enemy in a large ground battle with infantry companies and battalions that could be maneuvered around the battlefield to destroy the enemy. Sadly, because the enemy normally only moved in the open at night and stayed in the jungle during the day, these battles needed to be fought in the jungle where the VC/NVA had the advantage. In Vietnam, most officers at the rank of colonel and above never fought in the jungle. They did not understand the difficulty of fighting in it. Many of their orders were unrealistic, and led to unnecessary US casualties.

PART II

Victory

CHAPTER 10

Duty

And like the old soldier of the ballad, I now close my military career and just fade away, an old soldier who tried to do his duty as God gave him the light to see that duty. Good bye.

General MacArthur[1]

Like General MacArthur in his eloquent farewell speech to Congress, I believe we each have a God-given duty in life, and those who surrender their lives to God will be *given the light to see their duty*. This chapter will tell when and how God turned on the light for me to see my personal duty.

I received enlightenment at the age of twenty-six. Because it had a profound influence on my motivation and willingness to fight in Vietnam, I will present the personal background that led me to this insight and enlightenment. This background will also provide the reader with a better understanding of why I made the various decisions I did in combat.

In addition to testifying to the validity of Proverbs 21:31, this book serves as a testament to the validity of two excellent books which I recommend to the interested reader: Charles Stanley's 2000 book *Success God's Way*[2] and Rick Warren's 2002 book *The Purpose Driven Life*.[3] Both Stanley and Warren explain in great detail why it's important to find out God's purpose for your life and then follow it. They conclude that you receive power from the Holy Spirit to accomplish God's purpose for your life and for true joy. This chapter provides information about how, fifty years ago, I came to the same valuable conclusion.

In June of 1964, I graduated from Southeast Missouri State College with a Bachelor of Science in Business Administration. Within five months after graduation I was drafted into the Army and given the opportunity to become an officer by attending Officer Candidate School (OCS) at Fort Benning, Georgia. Although OCS added ten months to my military draft obligation, I accepted the OCS challenge and was commissioned an infantry second lieutenant in August 1965. I spent one year at Fort Hood, Texas and was sent to Vietnam in August 1966.

In Vietnam I led an infantry rifle platoon and an 81mm mortar platoon in the First Infantry Division. The nine months that I was on the front lines, the platoon I led lost only three men. Although I was wounded during this first tour, I completed my full-year tour in Vietnam, and in August of 1967, I returned home.

When I returned from Vietnam my draft obligation was over and I enrolled in the University of Missouri's Graduate School of Business. After one year in graduate school I became anxious to start working and make my fortune. I decided southern California was where I wanted to live and work. My goal was to eventually have my own land development company in the San Diego area and become a millionaire by age thirty. Because I wanted to live in the San Diego area, I took a job as a marketing coordinator with the San Diego Gas and Electric Company (SDG&E) in July 1968. SDG&E not only was a great place to work, it allowed me the opportunity to become familiar with the area. While I worked weekdays at SDG&E, I earned a California real estate license in the evenings and sold real estate for La Jolla Sales and Exchange on the weekends. Within a year I met my wonderful wife Joyce while working at SDG&E and married her June 7, 1969.

In a very short period of time after moving to the San Diego area, I had the perfect wife and obtained the jobs that I thought would eventually lead to a successful life in real estate development and to happiness (i.e. an expensive house on the ocean, cars, boats, plenty of money to travel, and a great wife and children to enjoy it all).

Although I had accepted Jesus Christ as my Lord and Savior as a child, it was at this point that God provided an occasion that helped change my perspective on life, as a result, giving me a life of joy beyond my wildest dreams. While attending a real estate cocktail party, I listened to an extremely wealthy and successful real estate developer complain about his son wanting to become a social worker in Los Angeles. This man was bitter because his son would rather spend his life helping poor people than taking over the real estate business he had worked all his life building. As I listened to him complain, I realized that this could be me in twenty years.

Obviously, the disgruntled father missed what was really important in life. I am sure the father loved his son and in the world's view he felt that he was providing the best thing for him; however, the father failed to understand that each of us is created by God for a specific purpose. The father's focus was on what the world considered success, rather than what God views as success. The Bible tells us that God's purpose for each of us is unique and different based on the talents God has given us. That means that all types of jobs and professions are necessary in order to satisfy society's needs, except for those that are harmful or illegal. Certainly, providing homes for people is a valuable service. The father's profession was not the issue, but rather his attitude and motivation.

To find God's purpose for your life, one must first acknowledge that we were created for God and to do His will—not the other way around. Then, surrender your life to Jesus Christ by focusing on how you can use the talents God gave you to best please Him, rather than for your own personal worldly pleasures. Ephesians 2:8–10 states, "For it is by grace you have been saved, through faith - and this not from yourselves, it is the gift of God - not by works, so that no one can boast. For we are God's workmanship, *created in Christ Jesus to do good works*, which God prepared in advance for us to do."[4]

When I came home that evening, the Holy Spirit led me to re-evaluate what really was important to me in life and instilled in me a tremendous desire to please God. I had a new desire to read the Holy Bible and find out what pleases God, as well as a desire to bring Him glory and honor.

The United Nations' *Universal Declaration of Human Rights* lists a number of human rights that all nations should guarantee their citizens. Because an individual's knowledge and faith in the one true God has eternal consequences, the United Nations' *Article 18* is the most important. *Article 18* states, "Everyone has the right to freedom of thought, conscience and religion; this right includes freedom to change his religion or belief, and freedom, either alone or in community with others and in public or private, to manifest his religion or belief in teaching, practice, worship and observance."[5] Jesus tells us this right is the most important human right when He says, in Mark 8:38, "What good is it for a man to gain the whole world, yet forfeit his soul?"[6] Other rights such as the right to choose one's spouse, government leader, or even profession, cannot compare to the right to find the one true God and eternal life. It is blasphemy and a lack of faith to think that God does not have the power to provide those He chooses with the wisdom to discern what is true and what is false. Therefore, no man—whether Christian Catholic, Christian Protestant, Muslim, Buddhist, Mormon, Hindu, or atheist—has the right to restrict another human's freedom to hear all theologies in order to find the one true God. Restricting freedom to seek truth is tantamount to brainwashing. Similar to most Islamic nations, communist nations do not comply with the United Nations' *Universal Declaration of Human Rights, Article 18.* Therefore, when communist insurgents or governments take over a country by force, they restrict freedom of religion and deny the population the opportunity to freely hear about Jesus Christ. Although many Communist and Islamic states claim to comply with Article 18, none fully do. Citizens within these countries are discouraged to become a Christian by denying Christians various opportunities such as schooling or certain jobs, and even in some countries by putting Christians in jail or to death.

In light of the above, I concluded that communist military aggression was a major threat to religious freedom. Knowing that citizens within a communist nation are prevented from knowing Jesus Christ as their Lord and Savior, and as a result denied an opportunity to receive eternal life, I decided I would be doing God's will in helping to stop the spread of communism or any other ideology restricting freedom of religion that is being forced upon people around the world *through the barrel of a gun.*

Even though three of my men from the infantry rifle platoon that I led during my first tour in Vietnam were killed and I myself was wounded, my platoon performed extremely well. I believed I was an effective leader and that I had gained valuable counterinsurgency experience and knowledge that would be useful.

God created each of us with specific abilities to do good works. Having served a tour in Vietnam leading an infantry platoon in combat, I was convinced that God had given me the physical and mental ability for military service. James tells us in James 4:17, "Anyone, then, who knows the good he ought to do and doesn't do it, sins."[7] Additionally, in Matthew 25:14-30 Jesus makes it clear that we should not be lazy, in the parable about a man going on a journey who entrusted his property to his servants. When the man returned, he praises the servants that increased what was given them and condemned the one who did nothing.[8] Clearly, God expects us to fully use our God given gifts to accomplish the works for which He created us.

Having served as an infantry officer in Vietnam, I knew firsthand of the hardships and dangers of combat; however, I also knew that Jesus tells us in Matthew 10:38-39, "and anyone who does not take his cross and follow me is not worthy of me. And whoever loses his life for my sake will find it."[9]

Furthermore, I believed that if God gives a person a particular duty to accomplish, then He will provide that person the wisdom and ability to achieve it. In Philippians 4:13 Paul says, "I can do everything through Him [Jesus Christ] who gives me strength."[10]

After discussing it with Joyce, I decided to go back on active duty and devote my life to fighting communism so that not only my future children and grandchildren, but all people in the world, would have an opportunity to learn about Jesus and receive eternal life. This decision was based on a love of and obedience to God, as well as a love for others - regardless of their race or nationality.

Within a few months of making the decision to return to the military, I was back in the Army, promoted to captain, and sent to Airborne School at Fort Benning, Georgia to become parachute-jump qualified. After graduating from Airborne School I was assigned to Fort Bragg, North Carolina, for a few months before being sent back to Vietnam.

The remaining chapters of this book will show the value of making career decisions based on what God wants you to do with your life, rather than on worldly pleasures. As evidence of the above statement the following chapters of this book provide a chronological description of the day-by-day operations of the unparalleled success of the infantry company I commanded in Vietnam. I believe God blessed the company with success because my motives for choosing a military career were pleasing to God. Moreover, when a person's motives are right, and one has faith that what he asks for will be done, prayer is extremely powerful. Finally, an account of my company's operations will provide the reader a view of combat in Vietnam different than the one presented by the media and other authors.

Figure 1: Company Vietnamese interpreter next to the CHICOM claymore mine left behind by the VC when Schmidt's LP spotted him attempting to set it up

Figure 2: US claymore mine used in Mechanical Ambushes

Figure 3: Alpha Company's APCs herringboned after one of
the tracks hit a mine in the road near Katum. Men of Alpha
Company cooling off the barrel of their .50 cal MGs

Figure 4: After treating an NVA soldier's wounds, the Alpha
Company medic compassionately gives the NVA a cigarette

Figure 5: LTC Schmidt with a Vietnamese interpreter interrogating
a captured NVA female soldier who was found hiding in a tunnel

Figure 6: Men of Alpha Company taking a much appreciated
swim in a B-52 bomb crater after a successful operation

Figure 7: Schmidt with some of his men hauling out 170
rounds of 57 mm recoilless and 17 rounds of 75 mm antitank
ammunition discovered in an NVA/VC tunnel

Figure 8: Schmidt holding 3 AK-47s and a RPG after a successful ambush
which resulted in one NVA KIA and two wounded NVA prisoners

Figure 9: Test firing a 7.62 Gatling mini-gun taken off a helicopter and mounted on an Alpha Company APC

Figure 10: Schmidt teaching the Mechanical Ambush to the 7th Special Forces Group at Fort Bragg, NC.

Figure 11: Captured NVA weapons and equipment from a successful ambush

Figure 12: Alpha Company returning from a dismounted search of
a marshy jungle area near Katum and the Cambodian border

**Fig 13: Helicopter extraction after a dismounted search
operation between Katum and the Cambodian border**

Fig 14: Just another day at the office

Figure 15: Something worth fighting to protect

Figure 16: Schmidt is searching the area along the Saigon River
that ran adjacent to the area known as the Iron Triangle

Figure 17: Vietnamese patrol boats picking up elements of Alpha Company. Alpha Company was used to search out areas along the shores of the Saigon River. The operation lasted only one day and had negative results

Figure 18: Alpha Company busting through bamboo during a search for NVA/VC base camps

Figure 19: Alpha Company Armored Personnel
Carriers staying off the roads near Katum

Figure 20: Shortly before retiring Schmidt served three years
as Special Operations Command, Pacific's (SOCPAC's) Chief
of Operations, where his vast experience in counter-guerrilla
operations was of immense value in the Philippines

CHAPTER 11

The Mechanical Ambush and the Automated Battlefield

*But whoever listens to me will live in safety and be at
ease, without fear of harm.*

Proverbs 1:33[1]

The most successful tactic that the Lord provided my infantry company
the wisdom to use was the mechanical ambush (MA). Information about
this effective weapon system is provided prior to the chapters which will
present the day-by-day operations of my company in combat.

A mechanical ambush is a sophisticated unmanned ambush constructed
of claymore mines daisy-chained or wired in parallel and placed along a
trail or location used by or visited by the enemy. Troops in the field refer to
these modified mines as mechanical ambushes or automatic ambushes. For
the purpose of this book, I will use the term mechanical ambush. In this
unclassified book, it would be irresponsible for me to elaborate any further
on the specific details of the MA's design and the various techniques used
with it; however, suffice it to say the MAs used during the latter days of
Vietnam were significantly more advanced than those found in current
unclassified US military field manuals.

What most people, including the majority of our military leaders, are
not aware of is how effective the MA was, and how much the US infantry

depended upon it in the latter years of the Vietnam conflict. The mines normally used were claymore (M-18A1) anti-personnel mines. The US claymore antipersonnel mine contains C-4 explosive behind a matrix of about 700 1/8-inch-diameter steel balls. When detonated, it propels these 700 steel balls in a 60-degree fan-shaped pattern to an optimum range of 50 meters and a maximum distance of 100 meters (See figure # 2).

Even though this mine is designed to be detonated by an electrical firing device (M57) actuated by the soldier employing the mine, soldiers in the field modified the mine so that it would detonate when an enemy soldier tripped a tripwire. Unlike most anti-personnel land mines that kill or wound one or two enemy soldiers, the MA could be constructed to destroy an entire enemy patrol.

During my first tour in 1966, when I was an infantry rifle platoon leader in the First Infantry Division, I employed a rather unsophisticated MA that used a mouse trap or clothespin as the firing device. However, MAs didn't evolve into an accepted method of conducting ambushes until 1970. During my second Vietnam tour in 1970, I commanded Alpha Company, 2nd Battalion (Mechanized), 22nd Infantry in the 25th Infantry Division. Not all units were using MAs, and the effectiveness of the MAs that were used depended on the skill of the unit members emplacing them. Fortunately, God blessed my company with two brilliant sergeants: Sergeant Henry Smith and Sergeant James McDonnell. Although most of the men in Alpha Company were proficient in setting out mechanical ambushes, these two sergeants were extremely innovative and in a league of their own.

My company's mission was to stop the infiltration of communist soldiers into the hamlets and villages, and to protect Vietnamese civilians so they could freely exercise their democracy and liberty. The MA provided Alpha Company the capability of establishing an automated battlefield, and of successfully protecting an area three times the size that most companies protected. The automated battlefield allowed Alpha Company the ability to maximize its combat power, while minimizing the risk to its own troops.

Because MAs allowed us to ambush deep into enemy controlled territory for long periods of time while protecting the United States' center of gravity by keeping US troops out of harm's way, the MA became our primary weapon system. As a mechanized infantry unit, we were able to systematically search large restricted AOs assigned to us, and at every enemy base camp we found, on every trail we crossed, a manned ambush or unmanned MA could be emplaced.

There were significant advantages in using MAs in this kind of warfare. Initially, senior officers assumed that enemy movement over trails could be stopped by manned ambushes. Unfortunately, most US units that were tasked to conduct these night ambushes were either detected or were not dedicated enough to the mission to go where they were directed. Consequently, this failure permitted the VC/NVA to move about at night with relative freedom, giving them an advantage over US and ARVN forces.

This freedom to move at night allowed them the ability to achieve three important Principles of War: maneuvering, massing of troops at key locations, and the element of surprise. The MAs, where they were employed, clearly denied them this very important advantage.

The MAs were extremely effective for enemy interdiction and attrition. Both the physical and psychological losses to enemy forces caused by MAs were significant. The MAs didn't make noise, fall asleep, eat, or initiate an ambush too early.

To avoid killing any civilians or friendly troops, it was imperative that MAs be employed responsibly. They were only emplaced in designated restricted areas and removed before the troops that employed them departed the AO. In my two tours in Vietnam, I emplaced hundreds of MAs. Not one civilian or friendly soldier was killed by an MA emplaced by my unit.

There is a notion that anti-personnel mines are evil and should be banned. In fact, anti-personnel mines, if used responsibly, save civilian lives and can lead them to freedom. All weapons used in war can be deadly and evil if used irresponsibly or by ruthless people. It is the irresponsible and callous use of anti-personnel mines that should be banned, not the mines themselves.

As I mentioned, when assigned a restricted AO, I would usually conduct patrols within so as to encircle the entire AO. On every trail that a patrol crossed, I would have them emplace an MA, thereby effectively killing or wounding any enemy entering, leaving, or passing through the AO. Then we would systematically search the area for enemy supplies and base camps. If an enemy base was found, I would have an MA emplaced to kill and wound any enemy soldiers returning to the base. The initiative in my AO no longer belonged to the enemy; the entire AO became a huge trap.

While Alpha Company operated in a restricted area, we usually had ten to fifteen MAs employed at all times. I required at least two soldiers to emplace an MA. They were also required to draw a detailed map of the location of the tripwire, claymores and battery in case those emplacing the MA were medevaced out of the area. Each MA was assigned an alphanumeric identification and the eight-digit coordinate of its location.

This detailed information on each MA was given to my 81 mm mortar platoon to plot and work up the firing data to each active MA. I plotted the azimuth and distance to each MA so that when we heard an explosion or saw the black smoke rising from the jungle, I would know which ambush had been detonated. Consequently, we were able to immediately respond to the site with accurate 81 mm mortar fire and troops on the ground. The mortars not only provided immediate indirect fire support for the troops on the ground, but they also increased the effectiveness of the MA by killing more of the enemy, and by keeping the enemy from removing weapons and documents. Because the impacting mortar rounds disguised what caused the claymore explosions, firing them into the area also allowed us to emplace additional mechanical ambush on the same trail.

The reason no civilian or friendly soldier was ever killed or injured by any MA employed by my company was because we established procedures and strictly followed them. For example, MAs were only employed after the civilian curfew or in restricted areas; two individuals were required to be familiar with each MA; detailed diagrams and grid coordinates of each MA were provided to the company and battalion headquarters; all MAs not detonated had to be retrieved when the ambush was no longer needed or if our unit was to move out of the area.

The use of MAs was not an established US military doctrine; however, its use demonstrated the effectiveness of flexibility and irregular actions in combat. Sun Tzu said, "Prerequisite for the exercise of combat power: The ability to exercise flexible actions in combat ... the armies' legions can be sent to fully engage the enemy and will never be defeated—through irregular and regular actions."[2]

To give the reader a better understanding of the effectiveness of the MA and the tactics used during the latter years of Vietnam, the following chapters chronologically present the events of my second tour in Vietnam from May 1970–May 1971.

CHAPTER 12

Cambodia

Even though I walk through the valley of the shadow of death, I will fear no evil, for you (Lord) are with me; your rod and your staff, they comfort me.

Psalm 23:4[1]

On May 16, 1970, I was back in Vietnam for my second tour. I was assign to the 2nd Battalion, (Mechanized), 22nd Infantry (2-22 Mech) of the 25th Infantry Division.

The 2-22 Mech, also referred to as the Triple Deuce Battalion, played a key role in the May 6, 1970, Cambodian incursion to clean out NVA/VC sanctuaries. Because I had to first in-process and attend a required orientation school for all new arrivals, it wasn't until May 26 that I was able to join the Triple Deuce in Cambodia

Triple Deuce's Cambodian Operations Prior to My Arrival

On May 6, 1970, the Triple Deuce crossed into Cambodia from positions west of Thien Ngon village in South Vietnam to destroy the NVA Base Area of the 95C NVA Regiment and the headquarters (HQ) of the 9th NVA Division. Other than losing two armored personnel carriers (APC) to mines, the 2-22 Mech didn't suffer any losses. The Triple Deuce claimed 4 enemy dead, 1,500 NVA uniforms, 1,200 pounds of rice, and 200 gallons of gasoline and kerosene.

On May 10, the 2-22 (Mech) moved back south across the border to prepare for another operation in Cambodia, and on May 11, they joined an operation in Cambodia to destroy the communist headquarters for ground operations within South Vietnam, known as the Central Office of South Vietnam (COSVN).

As previously mentioned, B-52 strikes in Cambodia were extremely effective because they were no-notice and the NVA didn't have time to move out before the bombs arrived. The excellent results of the attack on a part of the COSVN headquarters are a prime example of the effectiveness of a no-notice B-52 strike. Prior to initiating the ground attack on COSVN, at least four waves of US B-52s, with six bombers per wave and each carrying a mix of over a hundred 500- and 750-pound bombs, hit the jungle where COSVN was believed to be located.

When the infantry battalions of the 25th Infantry Division moved in and searched the area, they found numerous dead NVA, an underground hospital, a motor pool of trucks, a communication repair shop stacked with radios, caches of weapons, ammunition and rice, and a field desk containing a COSVN stamp. The official count was 146 NVA killed by the B-52 strike. After the heavy bombardment, the NVA headquarters, hospital, and security personnel who survived the bombing were either suffering concussions, unable to fight, hiding, or running. Consequently, when the 2-22 (Mech) searched the area they did not receive any resistance and did not suffer any casualties.

Ten days from the initial incursion, it was evident that the advantage the US had gained from the element of surprise was over. Although the NVA could not protect their supply bases, they were able to reorganize their forces and go back on the offense. Subsequently, most contact was NVA initiated during the remaining time in Cambodia.

On May 16, 1970, 2-22 Mech had road-marched into an area which became known as Ambush Alley to search for the elusive HQ of the 9th NVA Division. It was approximately eight kilometers northwest of Krek and the area was a thick marshy jungle area with a stream running across an elevated dirt road. The monsoon season had just begun and heavy rain turned the road into mud.

The Triple Deuce set up their night defensive position (NDP) or what mechanized infantry and armor units call a laager position in a large clearing near the end of the small muddy road on the evening of May 16. Unfortunately, the commander made the mistake of staying there until May 21, thereby setting a pattern for the NVA to take advantage of. Mechanized infantry NDPs, should be moved every one or two days to prevent the enemy from having time to plan an attack on the NDP or an ambush against units required to use the same route over and over to come in and out of the NDP.

On May 18, returning from another day of reconnaissance-in-force (RIF), Charlie Company was traveling on the only road that entered the Battalion Command Post (CP) and was ambushed. Close air support, artillery, and Alpha Company came to Charlie Company's rescue and after two hours of fighting, the NVA disappeared into the jungle. Charlie Company had 13 WIAs and 3 KIAs, but only found 1 dead NVA.

The NVA were now actively targeting US units in Cambodia, not only by ambushes, but also by deception. The night of May 19, the Triple Deuce's Operations Officer received a request over the radio for artillery fire. The coordinates were on a battalion position; therefore, the Operations Officer asked the individual, who spoke English, to authenticate. The individual responded with, "GI die."

On May 20, Alpha Company was ambushed while traveling down Ambush Alley, but only received a few men wounded. Most NVA ambushes were conducted by squads; they were able to slip up to the road, dig in, fire their RPGs at US vehicles coming down the road, and disappear back into the marshy jungle.

On May 21, the Triple Deuce began withdrawing down the muddy road back to Krek with its Scout Platoon on point. They hadn't gone far when another ambush was initiated by the NVA. The Scout Platoon suffered 4 WIA's and 1 KIA from RPG shrapnel. The NVA ambush quickly disappeared back into the jungle when the platoon leader brought in artillery and close air support. The battalion continued on after the ambush, and laagered in a small clearing down the road.

On May 22, Charlie Company took point and no further than two hundred meters down the road, they ran into another NVA ambush. They lost 2 APCs and suffered 9 WIAs and 6 KIAs.

Again the NVA disappeared when the close air support arrived. The burned-out tracks were pushed out of the road and the battalion continued down the road.

Alpha Company, near the rear of the column, had stuck several tracks crossing a small stream and stopped to wait for an Armored Vehicle Launched Bridge (AVLB). The AVLB was put over the stream and the column continued on. Within minutes, the Scout Platoon at the end of the column was ambushed. The Scout Platoon had 8 WIAs and 2 KIAs. As before, the NVA slipped back into the jungle when the close air support arrived. After the ambush the battalion continued to move. However, rather than stopping at Krek, the battalion continued back into Vietnam for a few days of recovery.

The initial phases of the Cambodia incursion went well for the Triple Deuce. Because of the element of surprise and the use of preplanned B-52 strikes on NVA/VC targets prior to conducting the ground attack, friendly casualties were extremely light. However, once the NVA recovered from the initial surprise incursion, they began to inflict relatively heavy casualties on the 2-22 (Mech). The men of the battalion needed a couple days of rest.

While taking the two-day breather on the Vietnam side of the border, Triple Deuce Battalion Commander Lieutenant Colonel Parker was replaced by Lieutenant Colonel Vail. After the two-day recuperation, the 2-22 (Mech) headed back to Cambodia on May 25. The battalion moved back to the same laager astride Ambush Alley that they occupied three days earlier. Within minutes after the battalion arrived, the NVA opened fire on the rear of the column. Luckily, there weren't any casualties.

The reason the battalion returned to the same area was because the AVLB that they had put in prior to leaving the area three days earlier had become stuck in the mud and was still there. Therefore, the battalion had to go back and secure the area while a Sky Hook helicopter lifted it out.[2]

Joining the Battalion in Cambodia

I helicoptered into the battalion laager on May 26 and was not impressed with the security of the battalion NDP. Not only were the security measures poor within the NDP, the ways in and out of the position were restricted to one road. Because of the marshy jungle on both sides of the road, a mechanized unit like the 2-22 (Mech) was extremely vulnerable to ambush whenever it was moving. It was no wonder that most of the casualties within the 2-22 (Mech) were suffered on this road, and why it was referred to as Ambush Alley.

The bridge came in three sections, so it wasn't until 1800 hours that the Sky Hook was able to remove all three sections of the AVLB. Once the AVLB was removed, we moved up Ambush Alley in drizzling rain at dusk to our new night laager position. The new CP laager location was out of the marshy area and near Krek.

LTC Vail assigned me the job of Battalion S-3 Air/Assistant Operations officer until a line company became available. Having served a previous Vietnam tour in both a leg and mechanized infantry unit within the First Infantry Division, I was surprised to see how poor the NDP security and defenses were. Only a few fighting positions were dug and none of them had overhead cover. Since LTC Vail didn't have a previous combat tour in Vietnam; I informed him of the NDP requirements we had in the First Infantry Division. I told him that no matter how tired the troops were, every night LPs were sent out, two-man chest-deep foxholes with overhead cover were dug, sectors of fires assigned, and claymores and trip-flares set out. Although this was LTC Vail's first combat tour in Vietnam, he was a tough infantry officer and knew how to lead men in combat. He had probably already noticed the lax state of security before I mentioned it. Within days he called the company commanders in and established a new set of standards.

On May 27 and 28, the line companies conducted more RIFs, with no results.

On May 29, the battalion had an NVA defector in a clean NVA uniform turn himself in. He said he was an assistant leader of one of the NVA security platoons of two companies from the security battalion of the NVA 9th Division headquarters. He pointed out on the map where the intelligence and supply branches of the headquarters were bivouacked, as well as the exact locations of the caches where their weapons and supplies were sealed in individual tunnels. Although we were suspicious that the man might be a plant, we planned a battalion-size operation to be executed the following day.

Because B-52 strike operations were never established in Vietnam or Cambodia to react to short-notice requirements from ground maneuver commanders, a B-52 strike preparation of the area could not be conducted. Instead only close air and artillery were used on the area prior to the battalion moving in on the morning of May 30. Alpha Company led the battalion into the area and immediately its lead track hit a mine and four men were injured. As Alpha Company continued to advance into the area they were hit by RPGs and AK-47 fire, and suffered five men wounded and two killed. The battalion found a number of huts hidden by the canopy above, but the NVA security battalion was gone. I believe that if a B-52 strike could have been obtained to first prep the area, the battalion would not have had any casualties and the NVA would have suffered heavy losses.

Sun Tzu emphasized the value of using overwhelming combat power in the following statement: "where forces overwhelm can be like a hard rock cast onto eggs."[3]

The Cambodian incursion was necessary. It destroyed a significant number of NVA soldiers and enemy supplies. However, some of the tactics used resulted in more friendly casualties than were necessary. When correct tactics were employed, such as using the element of surprise and preparing the battlefield with a B-52 strike prior to sending in troops, the results usually proved successful.

While in Cambodia, in addition to searching for NVA supplies, the 2-22 (Mech) was tasked to keep Highway 78 and Highway 7 open. This meant clearing the roads every morning before the US resupply convoys could bring supplies over them each day. This obviously set a pattern that was hard to avoid.

On June 1, the battalion's 4.2 mortar platoon moved down Highway 7 to set up a forward firing position to support one of the line company's search operations. At the location they stopped to set up their mortars, they noticed recently dug foxholes along both sides of the road. They called it in to the battalion CP and continued to set up the mortar firing positions. Within an hour, the mortar platoon came under fire from the wood line. The contact only lasted a few minutes and neither the platoon nor the enemy had any casualties. If it were not for the platoon stopping at that particular spot, the NVA most likely would have conducted an ambush on a US convoy or possibly one of the line company platoons clearing the road.

On June 3, the Charlie Company commander went on leave and I was given command of Charlie Company for a couple of weeks until he returned. I continued to search the jungle and rubber plantations in Cambodia for NVA supplies and bases. I stayed off the roads whenever possible and never set a pattern for the enemy to take advantage.

Using a mechanized unit against a guerrilla force required flexibility. There are occasions when it is beneficial to keep all the troops mounted. In other situations, it is best to dismount some infantry to provide advance, flank, and rear security when moving. If contact is made, however, it's important to immediately move dismounted troops back or move the tanks and tracks forward to maximize their heavier firepower. If dismounted infantry troops are to the front or flank, troops manning the guns on the tracks and tanks must hold their fire until their vehicle moves into a position where their fire will not hit friendly dismounted infantry, or until the dismounted infantry pulls back behind or adjacent to the vehicles. Infantry M-16 rifles and M-60 machine guns can't compete with .50 caliber machine guns and tank main guns firing canister or flechette rounds

Related First Tour Experience

The effectiveness of a tank's main gun in guerrilla warfare was demonstrated to me during my first tour in Vietnam, when I had a tank platoon attached to my leg infantry platoon. I was tasked to locate and destroy a small VC base camp that had been discovered by air. I located the base camp. It was deserted. I set out dismounted security and had the tanks button up and destroy the huts. I took the remainder of my platoon and set up in a Vietnamese cemetery to test-fire our weapons across some rice paddies into a jungle area.

We opened up on the wood line of the jungle and all of a sudden we started to receive a heavy volume of fire back from the jungle. Because I just happened to have prearranged that particular clump of jungle to be one of my target reference points (TRP) for the company mortars to fire, I immediately called for mortar fire. Unfortunately, the company mortar platoon failed to continually set their mortars on the correct TRP as we moved during the operation, so they weren't responsive.

I also called the tanks back from the VC base camp and put them on line to fire into the wood line from where the VC fire was coming from. The tanks didn't have flechette rounds, but they did have canister rounds. The tanks opened up on the wood line and within minutes, approximately thirty VC came running out of the jungle, crossing a road that separated the cluster of jungle from a larger jungle area. My M60 machine gunner who was covering the road said he knocked two or three VC down as they crossed the road into the larger jungle. Rather than checking for VC bodies at the initial contact, I had my small tank/infantry task force chase the VC into the larger jungle. Unfortunately, as the tanks crushed through the jungle, one of the tanks smashed into some thick bamboo which camouflaged an old dug-in French tank position. The tank slipped into the dug-in position, threw one of its tracks, and became stuck. It was already late in the day and the battalion couldn't send a tank retriever out to us until the next morning. I set up a perimeter around the disabled tank and spent a long night in the jungle. What I concluded is that APCs and tanks come with additional mechanical problems, but their massive firepower makes it all worthwhile.

Evidence of God's Protection

After commanding Charlie Company for a week in Cambodia, the battalion captured an NVA soldier walking down a road close to the battalion's night defensive position. When interrogated, he claimed to know where a large NVA underground headquarters and hospital complex was, and gave the Battalion Headquarters the location on the map. Unfortunately, to get to the area, the battalion would have to move down Ambush Alley. Because the road ran through a marshy area, tanks and armored personnel carriers were restricted to the road and unable to maneuver against the enemy; it proved to be an excellent spot to ambush a mechanized unit.

Higher headquarters determined that to locate and capture those in the NVA headquarters and hospital was worth the risk of moving down the road. As Charlie Company was preparing for the mission, we received orders to withdraw from Cambodia on June 13, and fortunately, the mission to search for the NVA complex was cancelled.

As we departed Cambodia, we received a report that a US surveillance aircraft which could detect the heat emitted from human bodies had flown over the road that we would have moved down to reach the NVA complex area. It had detected a large number of NVA soldiers stretched up and down both sides of the road. The captured NVA was apparently a plant, and although I had planned to conduct a dismounted recon of the jungle area on both sides of the road ahead of my track vehicles, and had artillery on call for both sides of the road, we still would have suffered a number of casualties. Our higher command apparently had not read Sun Tzu's warning: "Be aware of the enemy's potential for harming us when conducting combat: With regard to enemy subterfuge [deception]."[4] Certainly, higher headquarters' decision to send the battalion down Ambush Alley to look for the NVA command post was a bad decision. Thankfully, God is able to override bad decisions made at any level.

It was truly a blessing that the mission had been cancelled. As I look back at my remaining year in Vietnam, I realize this was only the beginning of God's wonderful protection. God is truly faithful to His word. As Psalm 91:14 says, "Because he loves me,' says the Lord, 'I will rescue him; I will protect him, for he acknowledges my name.'"[5]

Shortly after we left Cambodia and returned to Vietnam, the Charlie Company commander returned. As soon as I gave command of Charlie Company back to him on June 17, I was immediately given command of Alpha Company, 2nd Battalion (Mechanized), 22nd Infantry. Alpha Company had over 150 men, 22 M-113 APCs with a .50 caliber machine gun mounted on each APC, and three 81mm mortar tracks. Before I took command of Alpha Company, while it was still in Cambodia, the Company was ambushed a number of times by the NVA, and although the men fought hard, they suffered quite a few casualties.

CHAPTER 13

Tay Ninh Province

Seek first his kingdom and his righteousness, and all these things will be given to you as well.

Matthew 6:33[1]

It was while I commanded Alpha Company, 2nd Battalion (Mechanized), 22nd Infantry for approximately six months in combat that God clearly validated my decision to make the Army my career and to fight those who would deny others the opportunity to learn about Jesus Christ. Validation came by allowing Alpha Company to kill or capture approximately 60 NVA/VC without losing any of our own men. This success did not happen in just one battle, but over a six-month period of hunting and being hunted by an elusive and deadly enemy. Because there were fewer large NVA units operating within South Vietnam and the Army of the Republic of Vietnam (ARVN) was taking over most of the search and destroy missions, there may have been a few other infantry companies that did not lose any of their men during this period in the war. However, I do not know of any other infantry units that had the same level of success at stopping the NVA/VC as did Alpha Company without losing any of its own men.

As discussed in the second chapter, the Bible tells us that King Solomon asked God to give him wisdom, not to benefit himself, but so that he could lead God's people. Likewise, my prayers in combat were not for wisdom to benefit myself, but for God to give the men I commanded and myself the strength, wisdom, and courage to do His will, and for God to protect us from all harm and danger. Success of a combat unit is determined by how successful it is at accomplishing its mission with the smallest number of friendly casualties. God is always faithful to His word. God provided the wisdom and protection to successfully accomplish the mission that He gave me. First John 5:14-15 states, "This is the confidence we have in approaching God: that if we ask anything <u>according to his will</u>, he hears us. And if we know that he hears us – whatever we ask – we know that we have what we asked of him."[2]

The key words in the passage above are: "according to his will." I believe what I asked was in God's will. Because out of love for God and love for our neighbor (the South Vietnamese), we willingly risked injury and even death so that the South Vietnamese would have freedom to hear the Gospel of Jesus Christ. Having said this, I also believe that if I wouldn't have receive what I asked, then it was not in God's will, and God had a better plan for my men and me. Although this book will show how God disciplined the United States as a nation, it will also show how God provided the individual infantry company that I commanded in Vietnam with the insight, innovation, wisdom, and knowledge to achieve an astonishing victory over its assigned enemy. It will identify, on a day-by-day basis, how our God-inspired tactics and techniques took the initiative away from the enemy and resulted in victory. Proverbs 16:3 says, "Commit to the Lord whatever you do, and your plans will succeed."[3]

Subject of Christians Killed or Wounded

Although, I believe God blessed my company by allowing us to accomplish our mission without suffering any loses, other individuals and units may receive God's blessings in an entirely different way. Surely a Christian's greatest blessing are rewards that are waiting for him in heaven that will last for eternity.

It is imperative that I make my position known upfront so that there is no misunderstanding as to my stance on the very important issue of Christians who are killed or receive a disability in combat. Even though I believe the nation failed to win a lasting victory in the Vietnam War because of its disobedience, I want to make it crystal clear that I do not believe Christian troops killed or wounded in the war were the result of their sins. I am confident that God's love, blessing, and mercy is disseminated to his children on an individual and personalized bases. The Bible makes it clear that Christians may suffer while on earth;[4] however, our sovereign God will use it for His purpose. Therefore, one's death or injury in combat should not automatically be seen as God's punishment. In Vietnam, as well as in everyday life, individuals who love Jesus and are being obedient to His commandments, sometimes suffer an early death or disability.

Only God knows what each of us was created to accomplish for Him in life. The Bible tells us in Romans 8:28: "In all things God works for the good of those who love him, who have been called according to his purpose."[5] God created each of us with unique abilities and for different purposes.

How God blesses an individual varies depending on God's plans for the particular individual. Certainly, how long a Christian lives on earth is not an indicator as to how righteous or how blessed he is. Jesus Christ, the only truly righteous person who lived on earth, was only here for a relatively short period. Jesus successfully completed the mission He was sent to earth to accomplish and then returned to heaven. Because of Jesus' sacrifice, death has lost its sting for those who have accepted Jesus as their savior. They have received victory over death through our Lord Jesus Christ.

Acts 7:54–60 tells us that God allowed Stephen to be stoned to death early in his life because of his testimony about Jesus. His death has been an example to the world of true martyrdom in contrast to those false religions that would erroneously claim that a martyr is one who is killed, while killing innocent civilians.[6] All but one of Jesus' apostles were also killed for being obedient to God and witnessing to others that Jesus Christ is the Messiah.

Jesus tells us in Mark 8:35, "For whoever wants to save his life will lose it, but whoever loses his life for me and for the gospel will save it."[7] This does not mean that those who risked their lives and were killed earned salvation for trying to protect the freedom of the South Vietnamese to hear the good news of the gospel. We know that Jesus Christ paid for our sins on the cross, so whoever believes in Him as their Lord and Savior already has eternal life. Ephesians 2:8–9 clearly states that salvation is not earned,

"For it is by grace you have been saved, through faith—and this not from yourselves, it is the gift of God—not by works, so that no one can boast."[8]

Only our faith that Jesus Christ's death on the cross paid for our sins leads to eternal life, but this does not mean that there is no value in the troops that sacrificed their life or suffered a disability for Jesus Christ. Jesus told his disciples in Luke 6:22–23: "Blessed are you when men hate you, when they exclude you and insult you and reject your name as evil, because of the Son of Man. Rejoice in that day and leap for joy, because <u>great is your reward</u> in heaven. For that is how their fathers treated the prophets."[9] Even though the troops' sacrifice of their own lives for the gospel is not what gave them eternal life in heaven, it certainly earned them a great reward after their arrival there. I respect and admire these true heroes who died fighting for the Vietnamese's religious freedom. I believe God does as well.

Since a person, who accepts Jesus Christ as their Lord and Savior, goes to paradise in heaven when he dies, a Christian killed while doing God's will is certainly not a punishment. The parents, spouses, and children of Christians who died in Vietnam suffered a tremendous loss. However, I hope they are comforted by knowing their loved ones are in a much better place.

As indicated above, a positive or negative outcome of someone who is killed in war is dependent on the person's faith in Jesus as their Lord and Savior. Likewise, a positive outcome for someone who suffered a disability in combat, is contingent upon the person's faith in Christ Jesus.

Some suffering that we all have experienced is the result of our disobedience, and is our Heavenly Father lovingly disciplining us. However, much of our suffering is not because of our disobedience, but rather <u>to strengthen, develop, or position us for God's purpose</u>. The Bible provides an example of suffering that was not because of sin. When Jesus' disciples saw a man blind from birth, they asked Jesus who sinned, the man or his parents? Jesus answers in John 9:3, "Neither this man nor his parents sinned, but this happened so that the work of God might be displayed in his life."[10] Jesus then performed the miracle of giving the man his sight.

The book of Job in the Bible shows that it is Satan that tempts man to sin and not God. However, even though our sovereign God sometimes allows Satan to use suffering to cause man to sin, God will use it for His purpose. The book of Job also warns us not to assume that a specific person's suffering is because of sin. Job's friends made this mistake when they judged Job and told him that God was punishing him because he sinned. God said to Job's friend Eliphaz in Job 42:7, "I am angry with you and your two friends, because you have not spoken of me what is right, as my servant Job has."[11]

The Bible also tells us that God loves us, will always be with us, and in the end, if we respond to the Holy Spirit and not our sinful nature, the suffering can result in good. For God all things are possible, and we know that God sometimes performs the miracle of healing. Thus some who have suffered a disability may not find anything good in their disability, and wonder why God has not answered their prayers for healing. God may or may not let you know the reason why; however, it is imperative that you do not lose your faith in Jesus Christ as your Lord and Savior. Rather, hold fast to God's promises to us in the Bible, and know His tremendous love. The following paragraph provides examples where suffering can lead to good.

The Bible clearly states that Christians will suffer on earth for a number of reasons. The following are some of the reasons: To test our faith; to discipline us; to direct our path; to humble us; to get our attention by reminding us of our dependence on God; to instill within us empathy for others; to be a more effective witness of the Gospel of Jesus Christ; to develop character; to demonstrate the power of prayer and increase our faith in Jesus Christ; and to joyfully look forward to a new world and body in heaven.

Irrespective of who causes the suffering, we can be confident that since God has sovereignty over the universe, He will use it for His purpose. It is important to understand that for all things to work for good, it requires meeting the criteria of loving God and having been called according to his purpose. My experience convinces me that God and the Bible is always trustworthy. Even though we may not always understand why God is allowing our suffering, Proverbs 3:5 says, "Trust in the Lord with all your heart and lean not on your own understanding."[12]

To understand how suffering can work for good, we must put our relatively short life on earth into prospective when comparing it to spending eternity in heaven. The apostle Peter is aware of this comparison when he provides us insight into the subject of suffering and perseverance in 1

Peter 1:3-7, "Praise be to the God and Father of our Lord Jesus Christ! In his great mercy he has given us new birth into a living hope through the resurrection of Jesus Christ from the dead, and into an inheritance that can never perish, spoil or fade – kept in heaven for you, who through faith are shielded by God's power until the coming of the salvation that is ready to be revealed in the last time. In this you greatly rejoice, though now for a little while you may have had to suffer grief in all kinds of trials. These have come so that your faith – of greater worth than gold, which perishes even though refined by fire – may be proved genuine and may result in praise, glory and honor when Jesus Christ is revealed."[13] Paul is addressing Christians in this letter that are being persecuted for being a Christian; however, the reward for persevering also applies to Christians suffering the dangers, hardships, and even a disability associated with defending peoples' right to freely hear the Gospel of Jesus Christ.

In light of the above, it is imperative to persevere and not to lose faith in Jesus Christ because of a disability. The book of Job clearly shows why it is important to understand that one of Satan's schemes to tempt mankind to sin and to deny God is by causing man to suffer. However, it is also important to know that our sovereign God can use it for his purpose. Note the above quote from 1 Peter 1:3-7 tells us that the suffering that the Christians were experiencing was a trial to prove that their faith was genuine. Jesus tells us the seriousness of failing the trial and to disown Him in Matthew 10:33, "But whoever disowns me before men, I will disown him before my Father in heaven."[14] Therefore, pray that the Holy Spirit will give you strength to endure your suffering, wisdom not to lose faith in Jesus Christ, and courage to use your disability for God's purpose.

I've found, that the testimony of the Gospel of Jesus Christ by a military veteran who suffered a permanent disability while defending people's freedom to learn about Jesus Christ, is powerful and usually more effective than one given by a veteran who has not received a disability. In 2 Corinthians 12:8, Paul asks Jesus three times to heal his disability, and Jesus tells Paul, "My grace is sufficient for you, for my power is made perfect in weakness."[15] In other words, the physical weakness in a human provides a perfect opportunity for the demonstration of God's power. Regardless, our sovereign God is always right and will always make our suffering accomplish His purpose.

I will leave this issue of those who suffer a disability while serving God with Saint Paul's statement in Philippians 3:19-21, "Their mind is on earthly things, but our citizenship is in heaven. And we eagerly await a Savior from there, the Lord Jesus Christ, who by the power that enables him to bring everything under his control, will transform our lowly bodies so that they will be like his glorious body." [16]

The above discussion on the issue of Christians that were killed or received a disability in Vietnam does not provide the reader any information as to why the US failed in Vietnam. However, first and foremost it reminds us that there is only one way into heaven and that is through our faith in Jesus Christ as our lord and savior; and secondly, the importance of finding God's plan for your life and having the faith to do it. It is God who decides how long each of us lives here on earth and what He wants us to accomplish for Him. What God asks of us is to believe in the Gospel of Jesus Christ, to love Him and others, and do the good he has created us to perform. No matter how long you live or how much you suffer, if you have faith in Jesus Christ and use the gifts God has given you to serve Him out of love for God and others, you will be successful in God's eyes and experience contentment, peace, true joy, and in the end your eternal rewards that are waiting for you in heaven. However, 1 Corinthians 13:3 reminds us that our motive for doing good works must be performed out of love, "If I give all I possess to the poor and surrender my body to the flames, but have not love, I gain nothing." [17]

Second Tour Tay Ninh Operation

Once we were out of Cambodia, I moved Alpha Company to a small US artillery fire support base (FSB) called FSB Rawlins, located near the small village of Ap Phuoc Hoa. Ap Phuoc Hoa was located northeast of the major city of Tay Ninh and a few miles south of Nui Ba Den (Black Virgin Mountain), a large mountain that sticks up from a relatively flat area. The area between the city of Tay Ninh and the Cambodian border is Tay Ninh Province. During my first tour in 1966–67, the Tay Ninh Province sector was the site of the principal Viet Cong (VC) command center for guerrilla operations in South Vietnam and the central office of the National Liberation Front (NLF); enemy resistance was strong. Now, after four years of fighting in the area and the recent destruction of enemy supplies in Cambodia, the area was much calmer.

Having an opportunity to operate in territory that I had operated in during my first tour in 1966/67, I was able to evaluate the progress that had been made within a four year period. Contrary to the US media and some historians, it was clear that we were definitely winning the war in Vietnam in 1970. Unfortunately, it was costing us more lives than we were willing to pay.

The US artillery unit that had occupied Rawlins had recently pulled out of the base and was deactivated. Alpha Company was given the mission of taking over the base and securing it until the ARVN could take it over. Other than sweeping a few roads for mines, escorting convoys, and conducting local search and destroy missions, the only action we received while at this location was to assist an adjacent ARVN base camp that was attacked by a company of NVA. I asked if they needed us to come to their assistance, but they said they didn't need help besides indirect fire support, which I provided them.

On June 26, the Vietnamese base commander of the camp we provided with fire support invited me to their base camp for lunch. They were members of the Cao Dai religion, which is a combination of a number of religions, one of them being Catholic. Since it was a Friday, the Vietnamese commander and his staff couldn't eat meat, but they went all out for the lieutenant I brought along, my driver, and me. We were given a Vietnamese delicacy: chickens just prior to hatching out of their eggs. Not to offend our host, we all ate them, but I can assure the reader that I will never order this off the menu in a Vietnamese restaurant. The rest of the meal was quite good. We ate with chopsticks and every time my beer glass was down a quarter, they filled it back up again.

During the lunch, the Vietnamese commander gave me information about the VC in the area. He informed me that there were approximately twenty-five VC within four miles from their camp, and showed me their location on the map. I conducted a search and destroy operation a few days later in the area, but found only a few old bunkers.

During the mission of securing fire base Rawlins, I was also invited to have lunch with the village chief of Ap Phuoc Hoa. He told me the VC came into his village to try to recruit his young men, telling them they had to help the VC drive the American aggressors out of Vietnam. The VC propaganda was that the Americans intended to stay in Vietnam, like the French had, and that the Vietnamese government in Saigon was just a puppet of the Americans. Interestingly, the VC never tried to convince the young men to help overthrow the South Vietnamese government so that they could replace it with a communist one.

Unfortunately, some US troops did not present a very good image to the indigenous population; therefore, the VC false propaganda was an effective recruiting tool. Propaganda does not have to be true to be effective; it only needs to be believable. Unless US troops were trained to deal with the local population, as the US Army Special Forces were, US troops should have been kept out of the Vietnamese villages. If a village was suspected of having VC in it, US units could be used to cordon off the village, but a Vietnamese unit should conduct the search within the village.

I believe the US's information program was a complete failure not only in Vietnam, but also at home. The program was never able to convince Vietnamese peasants of the dangers of communism, or that unlike the French, the US had no intention of staying in Vietnam after the war.

On July 8, 1970, I turned Camp Rawlins over to the four ARVN companies who came to secure it. We moved to our rear area base camp Cu Chi for a two-day stand-down to give the troops a little rest and to perform maintenance on our vehicles and our equipment. Then we moved back out of Cu Chi to an area about three miles northeast of Katum. Katum is located approximately twenty-seven miles north of Tay Ninh and four miles south of the Cambodian border.

CHAPTER 14

Katum

For the Lord gives wisdom, and from his mouth comes knowledge and understanding. He holds victory in store for the upright, he is a shield to those whose walk is blameless, for he guards the course of the just and protects the way of his faithful ones.

Proverbs 2:6-8[1]

On July 10, 1970, Alpha Company moved northwest out of CuChi for the long trip to Katum. I was familiar with the Katum area from my first tour and as my company's APCs roared up unpaved Highway 4 northward from Tay Ninh, I recognized the site that I believe was one of the most successful US infantry battles inside Vietnam.

First Tour Experience

The battle took place in March 1967, during Operation Junction City, after US Intelligence intercepted an NVA radio message that indicated they were going to attack the Special Forces camp being constructed along Highway 4, south of Katum, with two NVA regiments. The 2nd Battalion (Mechanized), 2nd Infantry, First Infantry Division, to which I was assigned, was given the mission to protect the Special Forces camp from the NVA attack.

Seven months earlier, when I was first assigned to the 2-2 (Mech) as an infantry rifle platoon leader, the battalion was a non-mechanized infantry battalion; however, after operating as an infantry rifle platoon leader for four months without track vehicles, we suddenly became a mechanized infantry unit on January 1, 1967. Both mechanized and non-mechanized infantry have their advantages and disadvantages; however, having experienced both, I preferred leading mechanized infantry in the environment we faced during the Vietnam War. The amount of firepower and ammunition carried by a mechanized unit compared to a non-mechanized unit was significant.

By the time the 2-2 (Mech) was given the mission to secure the Special Forces base camp being built, we had received our APCs and were fully mechanized. Using the camp as bait and drawing two regiments of NVA out into the open to attack a US mechanized infantry battalion in defensive positions was a tremendous opportunity to attrite a significant amount of the enemy.

The defense normally has a passive purpose and the attack a positive one, conquest. However, in some cases it is better to take the defense in order to weaken the enemy. Clausewitz identifies the advantage of being in the defense when he writes, "The defensive form of warfare is intrinsically stronger than the offensive."[2]

The Battalion Commander's idea was to put Charlie Company around the Special Forces camp, Alpha Company, in a laager in a dried-up lake less than a half-mile south on Highway 4 to secure an artillery battery. Bravo Company, to which I was assigned, was to be placed in a dried-up lake less than a half-mile north of the camp on Highway 4 to secure another artillery battery. In this way, the artillery batteries could provide mutual supporting fire for each other, as well as artillery fire for the Special Forces camp.

All companies, as usual, had prepared the required two-man *Depuy fighting positions* with overhead cover, and emplaced claymore mines and trip flares around the perimeter. Infantry fires were interlocking and artillery and mortars were pre-registered. Sun Tzu's advice on defense was well applied in defending the Special Forces camp: "Take advantage of enemy vulnerability: act beyond enemy abilities—in defense ... defend and be certain of safety by defending what they cannot attack."[3]

Within two days, the two NVA regiments attacked the Special Forces camp being secured by Charlie Company and suffered a devastating defeat. It is not known how many NVA were killed the night of the attack; however, in the morning, Charlie Company piled up over 200 dead NVA off the battlefield. Charlie Company was the only unit attacked directly and it only lost three soldiers. Although Bravo Company was not attacked, we could see the NVA moving into staging areas at the edge of the wood line of the dried-up lake where we were located. We were able to bring both direct and indirect fire on a significant number of NVA. Because it was night and a relatively far distance to the wood line, the NVA were able to carry any of their dead out of that area by morning.

Clearly, drawing the enemy out of the jungle and fighting him on our terms was a more desirable tactic than searching the jungle for NVA/VC with large infantry units. Sun Tzu emphasized the value of terrain when he said, "The general who can assess the value of ground maneuvers his enemy into dangerous terrain and keeps clear of it himself. He chooses the ground on which he wishes to engage, draws his enemy to it, and there gives battle."[4]

The only thing I would have changed after reviewing the battle was the design of the Depuy fighting position. General Depuy was the commander of the First Infantry Division at the time of the attack, and he required all combat units to each night dig a specific foxhole that he had personally designed. Depuy's foxhole design required that a dirt mound be built directly in front of the soldier and that the firing port be angled so that the soldier could shoot the enemy coming at the foxhole adjacent to his position. Because the attacking enemy would be shooting at the same position he was attacking, the mound of dirt in front of the defending US soldier would give the soldier protection while still allowing him to engage the enemy soldier attacking the position next to him. The theory was for the soldier in the adjacent foxhole to shoot the enemy attacking your position; you would shoot the enemy attacking his position. This concept looked good on paper, but it didn't take the human factor into account. During the battle, quite a few US soldiers climbed out of their fighting foxholes and fought from behind their positions. In the heat of battle, they wanted to shoot the enemy coming to kill them, rather than the enemy attacking the man in the next foxhole. Consequently, they exposed themselves to fire coming from across the perimeter and shrapnel from above in order to see and kill the enemy coming directly at them.

After we returned to our base in Lai Khe, I recommended keeping the Depuy fighting position with the overhead cover and mound of dirt, but to leave enough of an opening in the front so that a soldier could still move around the mound to see directly in front of him. Apparently, the Army came to the same conclusion, because when I came back on active duty a few years later, the Army's official infantry fighting position was identical to the Depuy fighting position except that it allowed the soldier to move from around the dirt mound in order to see the front.

Second Tour Katum Operation in 1970

After arriving in the Katum area, we were assigned a designated restricted area of operation (AO) along the border between Cambodia and Katum that covered about 25 square miles of thick jungle. As defined in an earlier chapter, a restricted area is a control measure that restricts all civilians or friendly military forces from being in or firing into the designated restricted AO unless the commander assigned and responsible for it is informed. I knew that any people within my restricted AO, other than my own men or friendly troops that I knew about, were enemy. Therefore, I was allowed to employ MAs and tactics that would not only defeat the enemy, but also protect the United States' own center of gravity.

The Katum area was heavy jungle and thick with NVA. Shortly after arriving in our new AO, one of Alpha Company's APCs hit a mine in the road. In case it was the beginning of an enemy ambush, and to lower the chance of a direct broadside RPG hit, the other APCs immediately did a herringbone movement (alternating each APC in an opposite direction turn of 25 degrees) and fired into the jungle (See figure 3). It apparently was not an ambush; the mine only blew out a section of the track on the APC and no one was injured. Since the mine exploded under an APC that was in the middle of the convoy, we believed the mine to be command detonated. We found the wire that had been connected to the mine and traced it back to where the NVA had connected it to the battery. As expected, the battery and NVA were long gone. We were able to fix the APC and continued on our mission.

On July 24, at 1000 hours, one of our mechanical ambushes detonated approximately a half-mile from our company laager. I immediately fired my 81mm mortars on the site, and because we were close to the Cambodian border, I took two of my platoons with me to retrieve any NVA weapons, documents, or wounded. After setting out security, we searched the area and found one dead NVA and one live NVA who had crawled into the brush. The Kit Carson scouts who were with us tried to talk the NVA into surrendering, but instead of coming out, the NVA returned fire. My men reacted with a heavy volume of fire and once ceasefire was called, a Kit Carson scout went into the brush and returned dragging another dead NVA.

As I checked over the spot where the claymores detonated, I realized that since we had fired 81mm mortars into the area, other NVA using the trail would probably think the damage to the ground and vegetation was caused by mortar rounds exploding. I had the men throw a few tail fins of our exploded mortar rounds into the damaged area and had the two dead NVA buried a good distance from the trail. Because the trail came out of Cambodia and was heavily used, I had another mechanical ambush emplaced 200 meters up the same trail. By 1800 hours, the mechanical ambush we had just set out on the same trail detonated, and we recovered another two well equipped dead NVA.

On July 25, a recon airplane spotted two NVA taking a bath in a river approximately four miles north of our position by the Cambodian border. Alpha Company was tasked to check the area out for a possible NVA base camp. Because the area was marshy, I left part of the company to secure our armored personnel carriers. On July 26, the remainder of Alpha Company, with an attached Civilian Irregular Defense Group (CIDG) unit of approximately eighty soldiers, conducted an air assault to search the area where the NVA were spotted. Our LZ was a dried-up lake approximately 500 meters from the Cambodian border. I had the artillery prep the LZ and we came in firing. When we reached the wood line, we discovered NVA equipment and a blood trail. We followed the trail until it crossed the Cambodian border. With all the blood that had been lost, I doubt the NVA survived.

As we moved through an area that was covered in thick bamboo, I stopped the unit for a quick rest. To my surprise, the CIDG troops started collecting bamboo shoots and pulling out pots from their rucksacks to cook lunch. My most trusted and competent Kit Carson scout, who had once commanded a VC company before he became disappointed with the NVA trying to run things in the south, was also surprised to see how undisciplined the CIDG were. I told him that since they were attached to me, I wanted him to get them straightened out before they got us all killed. He gave me a big smile and within seconds he was in their faces. I don't know what he told them, but they had their pots back in their rucksacks and we moved out without a sound. We continued to search the area but didn't find a base camp. I moved the Company to our Pickup Zone (PZ) which was located some distance from our LZ and we were extracted without incident (See figure 12 & 13).

If I had the choice, I would rather have taken three of my best men and my trusted Kit Carson scout with me to conduct that area reconnaissance, rather than the whole company and the CIDG unit. I used every technique I knew of to prevent our being ambushed, but I knew moving my large US/CIDG force through the jungle could never surprise the VC/NVA in their base camp.

After our one-day dismounted search and destroy operation, we returned to our APCs and set up a new night laager. To keep the enemy off balance and to deny him enough time to conduct recons, develop a plan, move forces into the area, or dig in for an attack against us, I moved our company's night laager every one or two days. For security reasons, one should never set a pattern and never stay in one place too long. If you do the same thing more than two times in a row, you can count on getting hit by the enemy.

When moving into a night laager, I would immediately put out Observation Posts (OP) or Listening Posts (LP) to prevent the enemy from surprising our unit. I required my men to dig two-man fighting positions with overhead cover, set up RPG screens (chain-linked fencing attached to poles to stop enemy RPG anti-tank rounds) in front of each armored personnel carrier, and to set out claymores and trip flares every time we moved into a new night defensive position. Moving every day or two was hard work. However, Alpha Company's night defensive positions were never attacked by the enemy.

The policy of not doing anything the same way more than twice was particularly important when we were moving. Whenever possible, I always varied our route and stayed off roads (See figure 19).

While working the AO near Katum, we normally only moved three miles within the AO each time we moved our night laager. Camp Katum was a Vietnamese camp with US Special Forces advisors and it was located astride a major enemy infiltration route into Vietnam from Cambodia. The enemy wanted it removed. They mortared and rocketed it almost every night. Since we were only about three miles northeast of Katum, we were usually able to spot where the firing was coming from and to provide counter-mortar-fire.

Since we were located only a few miles south of Cambodia, there were a lot of NVA in the area. Between July 27 and 30 we had another three mechanical ambushes blown close to the border; however, we found only blood and drag marks. Alpha Company's mechanical ambushes used numerous claymore mines stretched out along each trail, so even though bodies were not found at these three sites, because of the amount of blood found at numerous locations along each trail, at least one NVA was killed and one or more wounded by each ambush. Working in our own restricted AO allowed us to develop some relatively sophisticated techniques for the employment of mechanical ambushes that proved extremely successful not only around Katum, but for future operations.

Alpha Company laagered overnight close to the Cambodian border on July 28. Prior to dark, all fires within the NDP perimeter are extinguished.

This night, an extinguished fire used by one of the platoons to burn their trash during the day flared up for just a moment. Within minutes, an AC-130 gunship that was flying over the area opened fire with their two 20 mm M61 Vulcan cannons. The rounds hit the jungle area only a few hundred meters from the company perimeter. I immediately called the battalion headquarters and told them to call the Air Force to cease fire. The AC-130 pilot said that he was not informed that the area he was flying over was a restricted area assigned to an infantry unit and when he saw the fire flare up he assumed it was NVA/VC. The AC-130 gunship is usually an extremely accurate weapon system; therefore, it was only by the grace of God that Alpha Company did not experience any casualties from friendly fire. I never was able to find out why this particular pilot had not been informed that the area he was flying over was a US infantry company's assigned area of operation. It was a major mistake or incompetence on the part of someone.

On August 1, Alpha Company was happy to receive orders to move out of the thick jungles along the Cambodian border and back to the Cu Chi area where the vegetation was not as heavy. We worked the Cu Chi area for a little over a week and then moved into an area west of Saigon called the Iron Triangle on August 12, 1970.

CHAPTER 15

Iron Triangle

The Lord is with me; I will not fear; What can man so to me?

Psalm 118:6[1]

In 1966-67, during my first tour in Vietnam, I conducted operations in the Iron Triangle, which is located between two rivers northwest of Saigon. At that time, it was covered in heavy jungle, and considered an NVA and VC stronghold. However, on January 8, 1967, the First Infantry Division, to which my platoon belonged, conducted Operation Cedar Falls. The operation resulted in an estimated 500 VC killed and most of the jungle cut away by Rome Plows (large bulldozers).

By August 12, 1970, over three years later, some of the vegetation had returned to the Iron Triangle. Still, the jungle was relatively light, and we experienced only light enemy activity in the area (See figure 16).

While in the Iron Triangle, we were kept busy conducting day and night ambushes. One night, I sent out two squads to each conduct an ambush on trails located approximately 300-400 meters away. At about 0100 hours that night, my men on the perimeter of our night defensive position detected movement to their front. To discourage any NVA/VC, I decided to wake everyone up to conduct a *mad minute*. In a mad minute, we fire every weapon we have out to our front. Since we were setup in a circle, it gave us a 360-degree kill zone. My company consisted of twenty-two armored personnel carriers with a .50 caliber machine gun on each and one with a 7.62 minigun (a small, Gatling-like six-barrel cannon) that we removed from a helicopter. Additionally, Alpha Company had four 90mm recoilless rifles which fired beehive (flechette) rounds. A flechette round consists of a thousand flechettes, which are small, dart-shaped projectiles. These flechettes are clustered in an explosive warhead that can be dropped as a missile from an airplane, or fired from a tank main gun or recoilless rifle. It is an extremely effective weapon against enemy troops in the open. When each man in a platoon's individual weapon and the company's twelve M60 machine guns are added to the above firepower, a mad minute looks and sounds like the Fourth of July.

I knew that if the leader of a night ambush patrol was not dedicated to the mission, he may not set up his ambush where he was directed. Rather, he would find the safest spot he could to spend the night.

First Tour Experience

I learned the above during my first tour in Vietnam, when I was a lieutenant and led an infantry rifle platoon in 1966. I gave a squad leader the mission to set up an ambush on a trail leading into the village we were securing. In the morning, the village chief came to tell me that the VC came into his village that night and took his assistant, who was a former VC, out to the edge of the village and assassinated him. The chief described exactly how the VC came into and left the village. I told him that couldn't be because I had an ambush on the trail he said the VC used. The chief insisted that the VC used that route; therefore, I immediately separated all the members of the ambush patrol and asked them individually where they had set up that night. Each man told me they set up in an empty house in the village and left one man on guard and the others slept. The last man I asked was the squad leader, and he told me he set up the ambush on the designated trail and the village chief was lying. Needless to say, the squad leader was disciplined, and I learned a valuable lesson in human behavior.

Second Tour Iron Triangle Operation in 1970

In light of the above experience, before I initiated the mad minute within the Iron triangle, I called the ambush patrols to notify them of what we were about to do. As soon as I did, the patrol who had just received a new squad leader earlier that month frantically shouted over the radio not to fire because they were set up just inside the wood line immediately in front of the company's night defensive position, rather than where they were supposed to be. The terrain around the ambush sites that his patrol was supposed to have set up provided protection and would have been safe from the fire of our mad minute. Because of this squad leader's failure to follow orders and set up next to the company's night defensive perimeter, his squad could have suffered heavy losses. It was by the grace of God that I decided to alert the ambush patrols before giving the command to commence firing.

For a unit to be effective in combat, the leader and his men must know the purpose of the mission. The Army's *Military Leadership Field Manual 22-100* states, "Leadership is the process of influencing others to accomplish the mission by providing purpose, direction, and motivation. Purpose gives soldiers a reason why they should do difficult things under dangerous, stressful circumstances. Direction shows what must be done. Through motivation, leaders give soldiers the will to do everything they are capable of doing to accomplish a mission."[2] I found that if the purpose of the mission was important enough to the troops, then it became their primary motivation to do what must be done.

I believed the reason why many soldiers who served in combat units in Vietnam failed to do the difficult and dangerous things required of them was because they didn't know the *purpose* of the war. Therefore, when a new man was assigned to my company, I would explain why it was important for the United States to be fighting in Vietnam. I would explain to him what communism was and that if North Vietnam took over South Vietnam, the people of South Vietnam would be denied the opportunity to learn about Jesus Christ. I would tell them that because knowing Jesus has eternal consequences, freedom of religion is the most important human right in the world. Additionally, I explained the strategic value to the United States of stopping the spread of communism around the world.

Most young men coming to Vietnam didn't even know what communism was or the reason we were fighting. If they were not told the purpose of the United States' involvement in Vietnam, their only objective was to stay out of harm's way and come back to the United States alive. We cannot expect our troops to risk their lives for a cause they don't understand. It was critical to give every man information about why we were in Vietnam, and also to let them know that God would be with them if they were doing God's will. It is critical for men in combat to trust in the Lord. Psalm 115:9 states, "O house of Israel, trust in the Lord—he is their help and their shield."[3]

I'm not sure if I had the chance to sit down and talk to the new sergeant who took out the ambush patrol about why we were in Vietnam when he first arrived, or if he just didn't believe what I had to say. Regardless, I did have a long talk with him after the incident, and I never had any more problems with him.

I did have one soldier who refused to go out on an ambush patrol. I gave him every chance to change his mind, but his position was that this was not his war and that his war was back in the United States.

It was a time in our history that the civil rights of African Americans were a major issue, as they should have been. Martin Luther King, Jr. rightly led the African Americans on peaceful demonstrations, and many good changes took place. Unfortunately, King's consuming desire for equal rights for African Americans clouded his understanding of the Vietnam Conflict. Rather than supporting, as a Christian pastor, the effort to stop the spread of communism so the Vietnamese could learn about Jesus Christ and receive eternal salvation, he openly condemned the United States' involvement in Vietnam. This lack of concern by King for anyone besides his own race and his speaking out against the war adversely influenced some African-American draftees well after his death.

Disobeying a direct order in combat was serious. I sent the soldier who refused to go out on the ambush back to the Cu Chi base camp to be court-martialed. Shortly after I sent the soldier back, I was required to come in out of the field to see my battalion commander, Lieutenant Colonel Vail. When I arrived in his office, the military lawyer for the man I was court-martialing was sitting in the office. The lawyer wanted to know if the man could receive an Article 15 instead of a court-martial. He said the man was sorry and wouldn't disobey an order again. Because an Article 15 is only for minor offenses, and at the most, results in a soldier being temporarily reduced in rank, I told Vail that someone else was required to risk his life to take the place of the soldier who refused the direct order on the ambush. It would set a bad precedent if he received anything less than a court-martial. LTC Vail looked at the lawyer, said, "You heard the captain," and dismissed him. The man who refused the order was sentenced to two years in Long Binh prison, and when released, he was required to remain in Vietnam until the length of his normal tour was completed.

I want to make it perfectly clear that most of the African-American soldiers in Vietnam did not share King's anti-war sentiments. In fact, some of my best and trusted soldiers were African-American. The above two incidents were the only discipline problems I had while commanding Alpha Company.

On August 14, I was tasked to conduct search and destroy operations by going up and down the Saigon River on boats driven by the Vietnamese Navy. I left a small force to secure our APCs, and the majority of the Alpha Company loaded onto the Vietnamese Navy boats and spent one full day cruising the Saigon River on the west side of the Iron Triangle. If we saw anything suspicious, we would land and check it out. It was a waste of time, but relatively relaxing (see figure 17).

Other than having one mechanical ambush detonation that only produced drag marks, the Iron Triangle didn't produce much. On August 20, we moved out of the Iron Triangle to look for an NVA 85-man artillery battalion that was supposed to be in the area, on the other side of the Saigon River.

CHAPTER 16

Cu Chi

Be strong and very courageous. Be careful to obey all the law my servant Moses gave you; do not turn from it to the right or to the left, that you may be successful wherever you go.

Joshua 1:7[1]

On August 20, we arrived in an area east of Cu Chi, close to the Saigon River, to search for the NVA artillery battalion that was supposed to be in the area. We found traces of a few NVA but no 85-man NVA artillery battalion.

After looking for the NVA artillery battalion for a few days, Alpha Company moved to an area northeast of Cu Chi and west of the Saigon River. This area didn't have thick jungle, but it did have a lot of enemy activity. I always wondered how there could be so many NVA and VC in an area that didn't seem to provide enough concealment. My question was answered years after the war, when I watched a documentary on TV, titled, "The Tunnels of Cu Chi." The NVA and VC had an extensive underground tunnel system in the area close to the village of Cu Chi that we never located during the war. In fact, the new communist government of Vietnam is so proud of the tunnels, they have made them into a tourist attraction.

We never found the large tunnel complex, but we did eliminate a number of VC and NVA in the area. On August 24, two mechanical ambushes went off within thirty seconds of each other. We immediately reacted and found a dead NVA at each site. Apparently, both enemy soldiers were traveling together, and when the first ambush killed one soldier, the other NVA ran and hit the second ambush. Between August 25 and 28, three of our mechanical ambushes detonated; however, they were too far for us to reach quickly. As a result we only found blood at each site and at one site, a sign saying, "US GO HOME."

On August 29, we apparently killed or wounded two NVA on two different infiltration trails. When we checked the sites where the mechanical ambushes were detonated, we found a large amount of blood at one site, and bandages and blood at the other site.

On September 1, we crossed a trail with fresh enemy footprints. I sent my tracker team and a security element to check out where the trail went. The tracker team consisted of six men, a scout dog, and a tracker dog. A scout dog alerts to the presence of an enemy from scent in the air, and a tracker dog follows the scent on the ground of an enemy. The team returned after about a half-hour. They looked like they had just seen a ghost. I asked what happened and they said that they were going down the trail when both dogs and almost the entire team without knowing it stepped over a tripwire connected to a booby trap. One of their last men hit the tripwire but the pin didn't pull all the way out of the detonator.

I took my most competent Kit Carson scout, the former VC captain, to check out the booby-trapped area. After searching the area, we found that the tripwire was connected to a 155mm artillery round. Additionally, my Kit Carson scout also found a buried US claymore clacker. A claymore clacker is a device which, when squeezed, sends an electric charge to an electric blasting cap attached to a claymore mine. If either the US claymore mine or the 155mm round had detonated, a significant number of Americans would have been killed and wounded. It truly was a miracle that none of the team set off the 155mm round or the claymore.

It is my experience in combat and in everyday life that the time of greatest value is the time spent with the Lord. Every night before I went to sleep, every morning when I awoke, and before every operation, I prayed for God to give us the strength, wisdom, and courage to do His will and for Him to protect us. If we do God's will, He is without a doubt faithful to His word. Prayer to God the Father in Jesus' name for the right reason is a powerful thing. I would pray prior to every operation, but once enemy contact was made, I was too busy orchestrating the battle to pray. However, after the battle was over, I never failed the give the Lord thanks.

James reminds us of the importance of our motives in James 4:2–3, when he writes, "You do not have, because you do not ask God. When you ask, you do not receive, because you ask with wrong motives, that you may spend what you get on your pleasures."[2]

After we found the 155mm round and claymore booby traps, I had them blown up and our own MA emplaced to eliminate the enemy who had set them out. By coincidence, I had scheduled a helicopter so I could reconnoiter the area. After the detonation of the enemy booby traps, the helicopter landed and departed with me on board. When we detonated the enemy booby traps, the enemy probably thought their booby traps had killed and wounded Americans and that the helicopter was evacuating casualties. When we returned the next day, we found that our ambush had been detonated. There was a large amount of blood with a number of drag marks. Apparently, the NVA or VC who set out the booby traps to kill Americans had come back to see what damage their booby traps caused, and then ran into our MA.

Counterinsurgency warfare is a deadly game of cat and mouse. To outfox the enemy, we studied their habits and patterns, and then capitalized on them. We knew the enemy used trails at night, so we focused primarily on ambushing trails.

After focusing on trails for a few months, while passing by night defensive positions that we had used in the past, we noticed the NVA and VC were checking them out after we had departed. The enemy was looking for information about us, old ammunition, food, wire, and other things they could use. On September 2, we started to emplace MAs in night defensive positions before moving to new locations. In *The Art of War*, Sun Tzu suggests weakening the enemy through enticement such as showing the enemy gains to lure them.[3] To entice the NVA/VC, we dug only one or two trash pits and purposely did not burn the contents we placed in them. We rigged hand grenades to explode if the contents in the pit were disturbed. Using the MAs in this manner was another example of using bait to kill the enemy.

At the first site, on September 2, we put rigged hand grenades in two different pits. In the first pit we put one grenade and in the other pit we put two grenades under the same object. When we returned to the old site the next day, we found that at the first pit the hand grenade was missing. However, at the second pit a grenade had exploded and we found a large amount of blood. I believe the NVA/VC were professional and searched for booby traps prior to pulling out items they could use. In the first pit they found the grenade and may have found one of the grenades in the second pit. However, after finding a grenade in the second pit they probably assumed it was safe and failed to discover the second grenade. Although we killed or at least wounded one NVA/VC, we realized that grenades were not the most effective weapon to use, so we switched to claymores.

Because the senior soldier in the VC or NVA unit checking out the site usually wants to be first at getting anything good left behind, the lower ranking men are put out as security. Consequently, we usually killed relatively senior enemy soldiers at the old NDPs. For example, I set out an MA using claymore mines before leaving our night position on September 3, and returned the next day to find that it had been detonated. There was an NVA bush hat with numerous holes in it so we knew it had killed at least one NVA. I had a tracker team with my company and their dog led us into the woods, where we found a fresh grave with an NVA lieutenant wrapped up in a poncho. In this particular MA, I had set up five claymore mines in a circle so to cover the entire night defensive position area; therefore, although we found only one dead NVA, there may have been others wounded.

On September 4, we heard one of our MAs detonate on a trail. I immediately fired my 81mm mortars into the area and sent out the platoon that emplaced the MA. As they moved towards the site, I shifted the mortar fire farther away. This tactic was used almost every time we reacted to a mechanical ambush that we heard explode in order to inflict additional enemy casualties and to keep the enemy from carrying off documents and weapons. It also allowed us to quickly shift the mortar fire onto the enemy if we came into contact with other enemy forces. This time, we found two dead NVA and two AK-50 rifles. We almost always found enemy weapons when we found an enemy soldier killed or wounded by one of our MAs; normally, though, the rifles we found were AK-47s. In this particular case, these two NVA soldiers were extremely well equipped and carrying the newest type of Soviet AK-47s. The fact that these NVA had new equipment and the latest Soviet weapons was significant information.

It was very important for us to keep the enemy from dragging off those we had killed and from taking away any weapons or documents they were carrying. In actuality, we were required to take a picture of all

VC or NVA we killed before we buried them. We would then send the pictures, weapons, and documents back to our division headquarters so that Military Intelligence could identify which unit the enemy soldiers were with. In the rear area at one of the higher headquarters, they had former NVA and VC soldiers look at the pictures and try to identify who a dead enemy soldier was and to which unit he belonged. Along with the weapons and documents, the pictures provided valuable information needed to put together the puzzle that would help our overall effort.

The following night on September 5, we killed another NVA on one of the infiltration routes. It was becoming almost a daily occurrence for one of our mechanical ambushes to detonate. This NVA was apparently some kind of carrier transporting money to one of the NVA or VC units. The squad that I sent out to respond to the MA came back with their helmets full of Vietnamese currency. I sent the money back to our higher headquarters with a picture of the carrier, his weapon and the documents he was carrying. As usual, I didn't receive any information back as to who he was, but a lot of enemy troops or informants were probably very disappointed when they didn't get paid.

Although, we were unable to find a dead or wounded enemy at every single mechanical ambush that detonated, I know of one for sure that was not set off by an enemy soldier. On that occasion, we reacted to the detonation and found a dead bird that unfortunately picked the wrong place to land. There was one other incident, on September 6, we found that one of our mechanical ambushes blown and the battery that sent power to the detonator taken. I'm assuming that the enemy soldier who set off the claymores was probably killed and that a survivor in his unit found the battery and removed the dead body and battery. If they had discovered the MA before they set it off, the enemy would not have detonated the claymores, but rather taken the claymores for their own use.

When we first started using mechanical ambushes, one of my major concerns was the possibility of the enemy finding an MA and taking the claymores and battery, and using them against friendly troops. To address this concern, Sergeant Smith designed a technique that allowed us to employ our MAs so that if an enemy found the ambush, they would be killed if they tried to remove it. No claymores were ever removed from any of our MAs and the only battery taken was the one mentioned above.

CHAPTER 17

Trung Lap

He (the Lord) will cover you with his feathers, and under his wings you will find refuge; his faithfulness will be your shield and rampart. You will not fear the terror of night, nor the arrow that flies by day.

Psalm 91:4-5[1]

Having experienced the adverse consequences of search and destroy operations during my previous tour, I always conducted search and destroy operations with overwhelming combat power, and did not pretend to be able to sneak up on the enemy base camp. As long as the ground was dry and could support it, I would use my armored personnel carriers and attached tanks when searching for the enemy's bases. If I had tanks attached, I would have them lead the way through the jungle. The tanks were able to knock down thicker jungle and detonate booby traps more easily than the armored personnel carriers. Additionally, when tanks or armored personnel carriers move through the jungle, they knock trees and brush down in front of them, helping to deter any enemy ambush. Depending on the area, I would have my infantry dismounted or riding on their carriers to keep any enemy from engaging the tanks from the side or rear. Once an enemy camp was found, I usually had the tanks run through the camp to set off booby traps and destroy any structures. I would have my infantry dismount their carriers, search the area, and blow-up any tunnels they found. Before leaving the camp, I would have a number of mechanical ambushes emplaced to kill or wound any returning enemy soldiers.

On September 8, we conducted a search and destroy operation ten kilometers northeast of the village of Trung Lap using the tactic described above, except we only had my armored personnel carriers and no tanks. We found the enemy base camp and as expected, the enemy left the area. Inside one of the bunkers we found nine 82mm mortar rounds, twelve 82mm fuses, and 360 pounds of rice in nine forty-pound bags. We emplaced our mechanical ambushes and pulled out of the area. That night at chow time, several MAs were detonated only minutes apart. A sweep of the area the next morning produced two dead NVA, one AK-47, and a map with valuable information.

Tanks and armored personnel carriers cannot traverse areas that are marshy or mountainous. Search and destroy operations in areas like these should be conducted by small five-man long range patrols that can sneak through the jungle without being detected. Once they find the enemy base camp, they can relay an eight-digit coordinate back to a fire control center for an immediate air or artillery strike. Most US infantry battles with the VC or NVA were enemy initiated, and most of the enemy casualties in these battles were by US air and artillery. Because small five-man undetected patrols can call in air and artillery, large, conventional-leg infantry-unit search and destroy operations are not usually necessary and should be avoided.

The following day on September 9, one of my Kit Carson scouts saw an animal snare in the jungle. We set out an MA. We checked it the next day and found a large amount of blood and drag marks. Because most of the Kit Carson scouts were former VC and knew the habits and tactics of the VC, they proved to be extremely valuable.

On September 10, the company participated in a *hammer and anvil* operation with the ARVN, which is an operation in which one unit (hammer) pushes through an area in an attempt to drive the enemy into a blocking force (anvil). The operation took place relatively close to the village of Trung Lap, so the area of the operation was designated a free fire zone rather than a restricted area. Therefore, mechanical ambushes could not be used.

During this operation near Trung Lap, our company was the hammer.

As we pushed through what was a lightly vegetated area, our Kit Carson scouts once again proved their value. To reduce the chance of concussion from the detonation of an anti-vehicle mine, US troops had sandbags placed on the floor of their armored personnel carriers, and the troops rode on top of the vehicle. Since I had ten Kit Carson scouts assigned to my company and we normally had twenty-two armored personnel carriers in the field, I had about one Kit Carson scout on every other vehicle. As we pushed through the jungle, all of a sudden, the Kit Carson scouts on top of a couple of the vehicles started jumping up and down, yelling, "VC, VC!" They jumped off the tops of their armored personnel carriers and threw open a camouflaged hatch to a tunnel that none of my American troops had noticed. They started yelling in Vietnamese for the enemy to come out, and when they didn't, they started firing their M-16s into the tunnel. We pulled out two NVA from the small tunnel. One was an NVA lieutenant who was wounded by the scouts firing into the tunnel and the other was an NVA woman. We learned later that they had just come down from North Vietnam about a week earlier.

My medic bandaged the wounded NVA lieutenant and I interrogated the NVA woman through a Vietnamese interpreter (see figure 4 and 5). In figure 4, notice the compassion on the face of my medic giving the wounded NVA a cigarette. Unlike some US combat commanders in Vietnam, I taught the men in Alpha Company not to hate the enemy soldiers, and that they were to treat them well when capturing them. Although Alpha Company killed more NVA/VC than most US infantry companies, I did not believe, nor do I believe, that any of my men killed any enemy out of hate or revenge. Although the VC/NVA were trying to kill us, I think most of us felt somewhat sorry for those we had to kill in order to protect the South Vietnamese. However, Alpha Company knew what the tragic consequences would be if we failed to stop the NVA/VC attacks against the South Vietnamese. Certainly, we wished NVA/VC aggression could have been stopped through diplomacy rather than war. Because the men of Alpha Company knew they were doing their God given duty, I believe they all returned home without any remorse. Killing to protect the innocent rather than out of hate or revenge, may reduce the possibility of a soldier experiencing post-traumatic stress disorder (PTSD) after returning home from combat.

Overall, US military units in Vietnam had a reputation of humane treatment of prisoners. This was evidenced for me when a VC soldier who turned himself in to my unit told me he walked fifty kilometers to find a US unit in which to surrender, rather than surrendering to an ARVN unit.

The hammer and anvil operation didn't produce any other enemy. However, on the way back to our assigned restricted AO, we came upon a B-52 bomb crater with crystal clear water in it. I set out security and allowed the men to take turns swimming in the crater (See figure 6). After returning to Alpha Company's AO, we set out MAs. In the morning, we found one dead NVA at one of our old laager sites. Because of additional blood found at the site, at least one more NVA was probably wounded.

On September 11, I had seventy Vietnamese soldiers attached to my company to conduct a search of an area five kilometers east of the village of Trung Lap. The area was heavily booby trapped; therefore, to detonate the booby traps, I called in an airstrike to drop napalm. It set the jungle on fire and one could hear numerous explosions. When the fire burnt out, we searched the area, but didn't find anything except a few old bunkers.

On September 12, Alpha Company moved back to the restricted AO to which we were assigned ten kilometers northeast of Trung Lap. While conducting a search back in our AO, we discovered a trap door to a tunnel. Concerned that it might be booby trapped, I had it blown open. My men thought they heard some enemy in the tunnel, but I didn't want to risk a soldier's life by sending one into the tunnel to find out. As per my policy, I had the men stick a bangalore torpedo in the tunnel and blow it up. A bangalore torpedo is an approximately five foot long metal tube filled with an explosive. It was primarily designed to cut through barbed wire and detonate buried mines; it also worked extremely well at destroying enemy tunnels and bunkers. In general, my policy was to never, ever risk any of my men's lives just to claim an NVA/VC body count. Every man in my company was like a son or brother to me.

First Tour Experience

I still resent the time when I was just a rifle platoon leader during my first tour in 1966, when my battalion commander told my company commander to have my ambush patrol return to a night ambush site to retrieve NVA bodies that we may have killed. At the time, my battalion was a leg infantry battalion, and we had been operating out of a dried-up lake in triple canopy jungle that we had air assaulted into, deep in enemy territory. From a helicopter reconnaissance earlier in the day, I detected a trail that led into the dried-up lake that our battalion NDP was located. The jungle was triple canopy jungle, which meant it had extremely tall trees and very thick vegetation. If a person was on the trail that I detected and looked up, he could not see the sky. However, from the sky looking down one could see the trace of a line that ran across the top of the jungle trees that had a little darker color than the rest of the tree tops. Because the NVA/VC probably thought the Americans could not see the trail and therefore did not know it was there, it was safe to move on. Thus, I thought this would be a good trail to ambush. When I returned from the reconnaissance, I planned and prepared an ambush for the trail.

That night I took out an eleven-man ambush patrol to ambush the trail. Because one cannot hear the enemy while one is moving, I would stop the patrol often to listen for any enemy movement. As we approached the ambush site, I could hear the movement of a couple of soldiers walking down the trail, and behind them I could hear a large group moving. We were still in single file; I passed the word back that no one was to fire except my point man and me. Because the jungle was triple canopy, I could only see a few feet in front of me. I was determined to let the enemy walk into the barrel of my rifle before firing; however, when the movement was only around fifteen feet in front of me, one of my men halfway down the ambush patrol file coughed! My point man and I both opened up full automatic ankle level fire at the movement. After I fired five full magazines on full automatic, my M-16 jammed—the chamber would become too hot and cause the ammo casing to expand and jam on the M16 rifles issued during the early years of the Vietnam Conflict. The close-in movement had stopped, as well as the larger movement further down the trail. I pulled my men back behind an old B-52 crater. Since it gave me some clearance from the trees, I threw four hand grenades into the jungle where we had heard the movement. I then moved the patrol back into the battalion NDP located in the dried-up lake.

I reported to my company commander that we had heard movement that sounded like an enemy force moving down the trail. Because of the cough, we initiated fire before we could be sure. Since the movement had sounded like men walking (rather than an animal moving) and because of the larger movement further down the trail, I was almost certain it was an enemy force. Regardless, I was not going to risk the lives of my men by sweeping through the area to see if we had killed anyone just so we could claim a body count.

Unfortunately, someone up the chain of command did want to be able to claim a body count. I was ordered to immediately take my patrol back out to recover any dead NVA. Even though I explained to my company commander that it was a bad idea to return to the ambush site, he indicated that the order came from above and it could not be changed. I knew if I refused the order, I would be replaced, and my patrol would have to go out anyway, but with a different leader. Consequently, I gathered my patrol together and we quietly moved out of the NDP.

As soon as my patrol entered the wood line, one of my men said he saw an NVA crouched down at the edge of the wood line. I moved back to where my man was and asked him to point the NVA out. He showed me where he had seen him, but said that he had moved. I threw a grenade at the spot. Unfortunately, it was one of the old pineapple grenades from the Korean War and a dud. I threw another grenade, which exploded, and we did a quick sweep of the area. After finding nothing we continued the patrol. We had moved approximately a hundred meters when the NVA opened up fire on the patrol, killing one of my men. We returned fire, broke contact, and moved back into the perimeter of the NDP. The movement that we heard at the ambush site earlier was certainly an NVA force. We probably had killed a couple of NVA, but risking our own soldiers to prove it was, in my view, criminal.

Regarding the problem I wrote about with my M-16 rifle jamming, I provide the following additional information: I wrote to the Military's Material Command about the problem soldiers were having with their M-16 rifles jamming when I returned from the field. I told them that I had tested the AK-47 rifle by firing over ten thirty-round magazines of relatively dirty ammunition on full automatic, and could not make it jam. I told them that I believed the reason the M-16 jammed and not the AK-47 was because the chamber of the AK-47 rifle and its ammunition had a greater taper compared to the M-16 round and chamber. Clearly, the more the taper, the more easily the round will eject from the chamber. The Material Command wrote a letter back, saying they agreed, but explaining that it was too expensive to change the taper in the chamber and the ammo. They wrote that instead of changing the ammo and rifle chamber, they were chrome-plating the chamber and slowing the automatic rate of fire to eliminate the problem. A later congressional subcommittee report asserted that the M-16 had malfunctioned "seriously and excessively" due to jamming. The report concluded that the jamming was happening primarily because the gunpowder that was being used sent an unacceptable amount of residue down the gas-tube recoil system to the bolt. The subcommittee said the sloppiness of the testing "borders on criminal negligence."[2] Was the congressional subcommittee's report that blamed the problem on ammunition influenced by various lobbyist? I do not know; however, I do know that a lot of American soldiers died because their weapons jammed while fighting in Vietnam.

Second Tour Trung Lap Operations in 1970

On September 11, 1970, after I completed the operation with the 70 ARVN, I sent my First Platoon to work with the 2ⁿᵈ Battalion, 34ᵗʰ Armor. While they were there on September 12, my First Platoon emplaced a mechanical ambush in the 2ⁿᵈ Battalion, 34ᵗʰ Armor's old night laager which successfully eliminated an NVA. The following night, they did the same thing at a different old night laager site, killed another NVA, and captured an NVA who was wounded from the MA.

On September 14, I brought the company back to Cu Chi base camp for a two-day stand down. That night I received a call that five of my men had been picked up by the military police while trying to sneak some prostitutes into the Cu Chi base camp. The men had taken out one of our armored personnel carriers and picked up the women prostitutes in the village of Cu Chi. I sent my executive officer to get them out of jail. Because they were all good soldiers in the field and because they had never been in trouble before, I gave them a stern verbal chewing-out, letting them know how disappointed I was in their actions, but handed down relatively light punishment.

It wasn't until seven years later in 1977, when I was assigned to

Germany and receiving my household goods into my quarters in Germany for a three-year tour there, that I found out the full story of the NVA money carrier that we killed September 5 and how that related to the men trying to smuggle prostitutes into the Cu Chi base camp. The customs sergeant who was responsible for inspecting household goods at the camp that I was assigned to in Germany said to me, "Sir, you probably don't remember me, but I was in your company in Vietnam, and something has been bothering me all these years. You know when we brought back all that Vietnamese money from the mechanical ambush that killed the NVA money carrier?" I said yes. He said, "That wasn't all the money that he was carrying. We each kept over $3,000 and it has always bothered me." I told him that although it was wrong not to have told me then, I commended him for his honesty now, and more importantly, that God forgives those who are truly repentant. I told him that if the men in the squad had asked me at the time if they could keep the money, I'm not sure what I would have told them. The money that the enemy was carrying did not belong to either the South Vietnamese or US government any more than it did to the men who risked their lives preventing its use by the enemy. Besides, the money we did send back was now in the hands of the communists. That seemed to take a big load off his conscience. I guess that explains why when we returned to Cu Chi, those five soldiers from the squad he was in had the money to hire the prostitutes they tried to sneak into the base. I didn't bring up the incident or ask the sergeant if he was one of the men. There were about ten men in the squad that retrieved the money. The $30,000 the men kept, plus the $20,000 I sent back to headquarters, added up to $50,000 being carried by the NVA.

CHAPTER 18

Ben Suc

Do not be afraid or discouraged because of this vast army.
For the battle is not yours, but God's

2 Chronicles 20:15[1]

Unlike leg infantry units that normally conducted a three- or four-day mission in the field and then returned to their base camp to wait for another mission, mechanized infantry units stayed in the field and only returned to their base camp for a couple of days for maintenance once every two or three months. On September 16, Alpha Company moved out of Cu Chi base camp and was assigned another restricted AO thirty miles northeast of Cu Chi and ten miles northeast of Ben Suc.

Alpha Company was given the mission to provide security for Rome Plows that were cutting down the jungle in the area. Rome Plows are large bulldozers. They operate in a group of five to eight in a staggered line, and cut down trees and then burn them in large piles. They can successfully level thirty acres in a matter of weeks. Denying the enemy concealment for base camps and infiltration was an important mission in counter guerrilla operations. Additionally, bulldozers were used to cut back the jungle from most of the roads in Vietnam to prevent the enemy from conducting close ambushes on convoys. Because of the three-day warning the VC and NVA received prior to B-52 strikes, my Kit Carson scouts told me they were more afraid of being buried alive in a tunnel by a Rome Plow than a B-52 strike. In fact, one of the Kit Carson scouts said that he had been buried in a tunnel by a Rome Plow and it took him three days to dig himself out.

To secure the Rome Plows required only part of Alpha Company to physically provide a perimeter around the operation while the remainder conducted recon missions to prevent an enemy surprise attack.

On September 22, we located a VC base camp during the day and emplaced an MA in the camp before leaving. We returned to our night laager, which was only 800 meters away, and within forty minutes after returning we heard the ambush detonate. We immediately fired 81mm mortars into the area and moved back to the enemy's base camp, where we found a VC with wounded legs. He said that there were three other VC, two of whom were also wounded. We searched the area, but had to return to our night laager because of darkness. The next morning, we returned to the area where we had wounded the VC to try to track down the other wounded VC soldiers. We saw numerous tracks; there looked to have been approximately twenty-five VC in the area. However, we didn't find anyone. We emplaced a few more MAs and departed the area.

On September 23, we started to use bangalore torpedoes for the MAs' explosive when employing them in our old night laagers. Since bangalores didn't have the large killing zone that claymores had, we were able to leave manned stay-behind ambushes to ambush the enemy carrying away any weapons and documents from our mechanical ambushes. The first night we used the bangalores, we also set out a manned ambush. When the bangalores detonated, they killed two VC; however, it was such a violent explosion that the other VC were frightened. They ran, rather than policing up their dead comrades and weapons. Because our manned ambush was prepared to ambush the enemy retrieving bodies at the mechanical ambush site, the M-79 gunner within our ambush patrol replaced his canister round with a 40mm grenade round. When the VC ran out of the area, one of the VC almost ran over our manned ambush. The M-79 gunner fired his grenade round at the VC hitting him in the back. Because the VC was too close for the grenade to arm itself, the grenade stuck in the VC's back without exploding. It knocked the VC down, but the heavy vegetation and darkness allowed the VC to crawl away.

When you command a mechanized infantry company, you realize that the enemy is keeping you under observation most of the time and can easily follow you through the jungle. Knowing that they were usually following us, on September 25, I put out an MA on the tracks we were making through the jungle with our armored personnel carriers. No more than an hour after I set out the ambush, it detonated. We immediately returned and found a dead NVA mortar sergeant. He had on him a letter to his commander asking for an award for inflicting heavy casualties on the Americans when he mortared their battalion headquarters a week earlier.

Because the NVA that was following Alpha Company was a mortar sergeant, he was most likely planning a mortar attack on our company. Killing him may well have prevented Alpha Company from suffering numerous casualties. This example serves to emphasize the constant presence of dangers that were unknown to Alpha Company, and how God intervened to protect us. It was as though God provided a shield around Alpha Company for protection.

If we are consciously doing God's will, we need not be afraid. In 2 Kings 6:16–17, the king of Aram sends a great army to surround the city where the prophet Elisha is staying, in order to seize him. When the servant of Elisha awakes in the morning, he sees the Aram army and is afraid. Elisha tells his servant not to be afraid because "those who are with us are more than those who are with them." Elisha then prays to the Lord to open his servant's eyes that he may see. "Then the Lord opened the servant's eyes, and he looked and saw the hills full of horses and chariots of fire all around Elisha."[2]

While in the field Alpha Company not only had approximately ten MAs set-out at all times, but we also employed two manned ambushes each night. Both emplacing MAs and conducting manned ambushes took men of courage. Unfortunately, sometimes one does not know how much physical courage he has until he is tested in a combat environment.

Alpha Company received a new infantry lieutenant while operating in the field. He was number one in his college ROTC class and seemed to be knowledgeable of infantry tactics. I assigned him a platoon leader position in one of Alpha Company's three infantry rifle platoons. Regrettably, after observing his platoon for a few weeks I noticed that his men were not performing at the level they previously had. Both my first sergeant and I talked with the men within his platoon and found that they thought the new lieutenant lacked courage. I already suspected the same; therefore, to confirm that the lieutenant lacked the courage to be an infantry officer, I told him that I wanted him to personally takeout the next ambush patrol. I told him that it was on a heavily used enemy trail, so I wanted an officer in charge of the ambush. The lieutenant turned pale and came up with every reason in the book as to why his platoon sergeant should take it out rather than himself. Although, he did not refuse to lead the ambush patrol, it was obvious to my first sergeant and me that he had no business being an infantry officer and leading men in combat.

To be effective in combat, leaders must not only be competent, but they must be respected by their men. Therefore, it is imperative for combat leaders to demonstrate both moral and physical courage. Because the lieutenant lacked physical courage, I requested that he be assigned to a noncombat unit and that the Army change his branch to a noncombat arms one. The lieutenant was reassigned to a rear area unit for the remainder of his tour and performed well.

The VC also had a practice of sneaking up to our night defensive positions and turning around the claymore mines we set out at night. On the night of September 26, we set out an MA along with our claymores and killed a VC trying to turn around one of our claymores.

On September 28, we located a tunnel that was exposed by the bulldozers and found a large cache of enemy ammunition. We found 170 rounds of 57mm recoilless and 17 rounds of 75mm recoilless anti-tank ammunition (See figure 7).

After we blew up the enemy ammunition, we stopped by one of our old night defensive positions where we had emplaced an MA. We discovered the ambush had killed two VC.

On October 1, we killed one VC by using an MA at an old night defensive position, and again on October 2, we had another mechanical ambush kill a VC at another old night laager position.

On October 8, the Battalion Scout platoon asked if we could show them how to use mechanical ambushes. I sent my best man, Sergeant Smith, for the job. The MA that Sergeant Smith set out as a demonstration killed three NVA and wounded another NVA, whom we took prisoner.

On October 13, we killed another VC using a mechanical ambush in an old night laager.

On October 19, we set up an MA on a trail that killed one NVA and wounded another two NVA, whom we took prisoner. Additionally, we found one RPG launcher with RPG anti-tank rockets, and three AK-47s (see figure 8). One of the prisoners said he was part of a nine-man squad that came from an NVA unit of approximately 100 soldiers only twenty minutes away. I maneuvered the company in the direction of the 100-man unit and emplaced another MA on a trail that we crossed. On October 21, it detonated and we found two dead NVA.

On October 24, we killed another NVA using a trail with a MA. A few days later, we received word that the NVA we had killed had been identified from the picture we sent back as a notorious assassin in the Saigon area.

I believe the phenomenal success and protection Alpha Company experienced was the result of Christ's divine intervention, and nothing less than a miracle. This experience of God's divine power deepened my faith in God's power and protection, as it did David when he fought Goliath. When he was only a boy, David had the courage to fight the Philistine's giant champion, Goliath, because he had previously experienced God's power and faithfulness when, as a shepherd, David killed a lion and a bear. David tells King Saul in 1 Samuel 17:37, "The Lord who delivered me from the paw of the lion and the paw of the bear will deliver me from the hand of this Philistine."[3]

Years later in life, as a Special Forces Officer, I would not have had the courage to do many of the things I did if I had not truly believed in Jesus Christ's loving faithfulness and power. When I look back at my past experiences, I clearly see how God compassionately nurtured my spiritual development and confidence in His overriding power as He did King David.

October 26, I received a message in the field that I was the father of a baby girl born October 24. Unfortunately I wouldn't be able to hold my little girl for another six months. Regardless, I was a very happy new dad.

CHAPTER 19

Alpha Company's Deactivation

The Lord has driven out before you great and powerful nations; to this day no one has been able to withstand you. One of you routs a thousand, because the Lord your God fights for you, just as he promised. So be very careful to love the Lord your God.

Joshua 23:9-11 [1]

On November 2, I brought my company in out of the field for the last time. President Nixon's Vietnamization concept of turning over the fighting by US ground troops to the Vietnamese was halfway completed, and it was now time for the 2nd Battalion (Mechanized) 22nd Infantry to depart Vietnam. Instead of sending the entire battalion back to Hawaii, the unit's equipment was turned over to the Vietnamese, most of the troops were reassigned to other US units still operational within Vietnam, and only the battalion colors returned to Hawaii.

I do not know of another infantry company in the Vietnam War that killed or captured as many enemy soldiers as Alpha Company without losing any of its own soldiers, I truly believe that God provided the men of Alpha Company with the wisdom to defeat the enemy, and that He protected them from harm. Therefore, in our closing troop formation, we thanked God for Alpha Company's success, and gave Him all the honor and glory.

Having made the above statement, I am not suggesting that units that lost men during combat were less faithful at doing Christ Jesus' will. I ask the reader to please see the thirteenth chapter titled Tay Ninh Province of this book on my position on this important subject.

During my first tour in Vietnam, I think we were doing God's will, yet I lost three outstanding soldiers from my platoon in combat. I cannot judge what is in one's heart; however, I believe all three of these brave men believed in Jesus Christ as their savior and are in heaven. However, this being said, experiencing the loss of men in combat, makes a person more aware of the importance of sharing the Gospel of Jesus Christ with others. For, it is **only** by God's grace, through faith in the Gospel of Jesus Christ that we receive eternal life in heaven as explained below.

The Holy Scriptures make it clear that because God is just and righteous, He will only allow a person who is completely without sin to receive eternal life in heaven. Since, all have sinned, none of us are worthy of eternal life in heaven, but rather are justly destined for eternal punishment. Those that think they can enter heaven if their good works outweigh their sins are terribly mistaken. There is value in doing good works out of love; however, the penalty of our sins cannot be paid by our good works. Fortunately, God loves us so much that He sent His own sinless Son (Jesus Christ) to be an acceptable atoning sacrifice for the remission of mankind's sins. Out of love for man, this sacrifice was achieved by Jesus when He took our sins upon Himself and willingly allowed himself to be crucified on the cross as punishment for our sins, and on the third day was raise to life. It should be noted that the Old Testament period animal blood sacrifices that were given every year were symbolical punishments, whereas the penalty for man's sins were actually paid for in full by Jesus Christ's once-for-all sacrifice on the cross. However, only those who believe that their sins have been washed away by the shed blood of Jesus, can receive this free gift. Because Jesus died to pay the penalty for our sin, the perfect righteous life that Jesus lived has been imputed or credited to us who believe. Therefore, those that believe have been reconciled to God, and are considered righteous and justified in God's sight. Consequently, we are saved by God's grace, through our faith in Jesus Christ and not by our good works!

It is vitally important that our troops as well as all mankind understand that all have sinned and are in need of a savior. In light of the above, there is only one savior and that is Jesus Christ. When Jesus told His disciples that He would be going to the Father in heaven, and that they will follow

Him later. It states in the book of John 14:5-6, "Thomas said to him, 'Lord, we don't know where you are going, so how can we know the way?' Jesus answered, 'I am the way and the truth and the life. <u>No one comes to the Father except through me.</u>"[2] Consequently, faith in Jesus Christ as our Lord and Savior is the <u>only way</u> to receive eternal life in heaven.

After Deactivation

After the deactivation of Alpha Company, the members of the company fell into two groups. If a soldier had less than two months remaining on his tour he was sent home early. Those who had more than two months were reassigned to other US units within Vietnam. I was reassigned to the 1st Battalion (Mechanized), 5th Infantry of the 25th Division.

Apparently, Alpha Company's success in the field and high morale was well known within the 25th Infantry Division. I was not aware of Alpha Company's reputation until I arrived at the 1-5 (Mech) and I was introduced to a 25th Infantry Division chaplain, who was visiting the battalion. When he heard my name, he said that he had heard about my company at a chaplain's conference held in Saigon. He said another chaplain within the 25th Infantry Division addressed the conference and said that he visited most of the units within the 25th Infantry Division and found that Alpha Company's morale was extremely high and that the troop's attitude towards America's mission was more positive than in other units.

It is a humbling experience to be entrusted with the lives of men in combat. It is a tremendous responsibility and one that I did not take lightly. Understanding that true wisdom and protection comes from God, I stayed in continuous contact with our Heavenly Father through Jesus Christ, and asked Him for wisdom and protection for Alpha Company. The Lord knows the motives of what is in men's hearts; consequently, He provided the men of Alpha Company with protection and success.

God blessed Alpha Company with extremely competent and intelligent soldiers; I was able to use the *participating leadership style*, or what the business community calls *participatory management*, when determining what to do and how to do it. Although I made the final decision, asking my subordinates for information and recommendations provided Alpha Company with valuable initiatives that led to remarkable successes not experienced by other units. For example using a helicopter Gatling gun on an APC rather than the standard .50 cal. machine gun was an innovation from one of my troops (See figure 9). Additionally, when troops participated in decisions, they tended to support the final decisions, regardless if it was the position they suggested.

Lieutenant Colonel Vail, the 2-22 (Mech) commander, realized the importance of the participating leadership style used within Alpha Company in Keith Nolan's book, *Into Cambodia: Spring Campaign, Summer Offensive 1970*: "Vail was happy to welcome aboard Captain Jim Schmidt, a quiet, mature, competent veteran of a previous tour. This tall, blond-haired captain won his grunts' respect by being completely involved with them, asking their opinions and explaining why he did what he did, so Alpha Company ... continued to be the company Vail could always count on to come through."[3]

In addition to asking for my men's opinions, I explained to them why I did what I did. Explaining the reason for specific operations included providing the men with the purpose of our overall involvement in Vietnam. I think most of the men believed that they were fighting to provide the South Vietnamese with the freedom to know and worship Jesus Christ; this had a powerful positive impact on their attitude towards the mission.

Sometimes our leaders forget that when we go to war, we not only ask our men to risk their lives, but also require them to kill other humans. It is imperative that our objective for going to war is a righteous one, approved by God, and that our soldiers know and believe this. If infantry soldiers know the purpose and importance of their mission, which is to find and eliminate the enemy in order to protect the innocent, then their motive for killing the enemy becomes one of duty, not hatred. As I have stated earlier in this book, it is my opinion that hatred and revenge are not necessary, and have no place in combat. There is a vast difference between the lasting effects on a soldier for killing out of hate and for killing to defend the innocent. Military and civilian leaders must understand this when motivating men in combat.

Similarly, because my lieutenants and sergeants supported the goal of defeating the communists in order to allow the Vietnamese the freedom to know Jesus Christ, I was able to employ the delegating leadership style as well. This allowed me to delegate smaller AOs within Alpha Company's larger AO to the platoons; thereby, increasing the area that we could effectively control.[4]

CHAPTER 20

Special Task Force

No one will be able to stand up against you all the days of your life. As I was with Moses, so I will be with you; I will never leave you nor forsake you.

Joshua 1:5[1]

The Battalion Commander of 1-5 (Mech) was an excellent commander and a Rhodes Scholar, but his battalion had not killed or captured hardly any NVA/VC. While at the same time the battalion was continually losing men to booby traps, mines, ambushes, and sniper fire.

When I first arrived to the 1-5 (Mech) I was assigned the position of Assistant Operations Officer (Asst. S3) and was heavily involved in planning and directing the day-to-day combat operations. I told the Battalion Commander about the success my company had with the use of mechanical ambushes and asked if they had used them. He said the scout platoon started to use them, but their platoon sergeant was killed while setting a mechanical ambush out, and after that no other unit within his battalion had attempted to use them. I told him that mechanical ambushes were extremely safe as long as one followed the correct steps while emplacing them. The Battalion Commander asked if I would give a class to the scout platoon on mechanical ambushes, and of course, I said yes.

The scout platoon was initially hesitant to have anything to do with mechanical ambushes; however, after I gave them a class and demonstration, they became more receptive. After the class, the Battalion Commander told me to take command of a small task force consisting of the Scout Platoon and Flame Platoon and show them how to employ the mechanical ambush in the field. He asked if I wanted anything else and I told him I would like one 81mm mortar section that could fire immediately into the area of any mechanical ambush we employed. He attached a mechanized 81mm mortar section to the task force and assigned to my small seven APC task force our own restricted AO. The AO was southeast of Saigon, between Phu My and the coast.

The leaders of the Scout Platoon and Flame Platoon were both extremely competent lieutenants and their platoons were well trained. We moved into our AO on December 12, 1970, and I started emplacing MAs on the trails in the AO. However, because the AO wasn't astride any major NVA infiltration route, we didn't have any results from the ambushes set up on trails. I assumed we were being kept under observation by local VC and they were staying off the trails in the area. The only activity we encountered was some harassing fire from the wood line during one of the nights.

As I had done when I commanded my company, I moved the task force's laager every one or two days. Assuming the local VC were following us, I emplaced an MA within the perimeter of a laager site as we were evacuating it. We moved to another laager only a few kilometers away. I had the 81mm mortar section lay their mortar on the old site and told them to have a man watch in the direction of the site for black smoke. It was only about an hour later that we heard the explosion and saw the black smoke rising from the old site. I immediately requested permission to fire the 81mm mortar and sent two of the Scout Platoon squads mounted on their armored personnel carriers to sweep back through the site.

The Battalion Commander was airborne with his helicopter at the time. He picked me up so we could fly over the area. By the time we arrived over the old site, the two APCs from the Scout Platoon were already there. The men from the platoon were waving two AK-47s in the air and we could see two dead VC. Apparently there were three VC who came to the site, because the following day, a VC soldier went to the village of Phu My and surrendered. He said that his two comrades were killed by a large US explosion and that he had enough of the war.

The Battalion Commander was so pleased with the success of my small task force that he wanted to give me one of his line companies to command. He asked the battalion S3 how much *command time* I already had in Vietnam and the S3 told him six months. The battalion already had six or seven infantry captains who didn't have any combat command and they were begging for a chance to command an infantry company in combat. Additionally, the three current company commanders had only been in command for a little over a month; therefore, the Battalion Commander didn't pursue the issue any further. The decision was in God's hands; therefore, I was content to do my best in whatever job I was given.

CHAPTER 21

Teaching Mechanical Ambushes

Now to Him who is able to do far more abundantly beyond all that we ask or think, according to the power that works within us.

Ephesians 3:20[1]

December 29, 1970 I went on a two week Rest and Recreation (R&R) in Hawaii with my wife Joyce. We had a fantastic time and it was certainly hard to return to Vietnam.

After I returned from R&R, the Battalion Commander assigned me to the position of Battalion S4 (Logistics Officer). This allowed me to be off line, but because we would be standing down the battalion soon, it would become one of the most important and hardest jobs in the battalion.

The fact that most of the NVA/VC now being killed by ground forces were killed from mechanical ambushes finally caught the attention of II Field Force, Vietnam (II FFV) headquarters. Although I was now a battalion S4 in the 1-5 (Mech), because of the astounding success that Alpha Company, 2-22 (Mech) had attained when I commanded it, I was tasked to teach a class to some of the senior officers within the II FFV headquarters on MAs.

On January 12, 1971, I gave a two-hour class and demonstration out in the field to Major General Wagstaff and Brigadier General Roberts on MAs. General Wagstaff was so impressed with the concept and class that he told me he was going to recommend Lieutenant General Davidson, the II FFV Commander to attend my class.

I never did give General Davidson a class, but II FFV tasked me to give a class on MAs on January 20 to approximately forty Vietnamese officers from the 5th ARVN Cavalry Brigade before they conducted an incursion into Cambodia. I presented the class to the ARVN using a Vietnamese interpreter, and it went extremely well. Because there was always the danger of ARVN units being infiltrated with VC spies, and to protect US troops, I didn't teach the ARVN the classified techniques we used to keep the NVA/VC from stealing our MA claymores if they were discovered.

On February 4, 1971, Major General Wagstaff wanted me to teach all the Vietnamese forces in Binh Doung Province on how to use MAs. I believed the Vietnamese needed to know how to employ mechanical ambushes in order to win the war; I would have liked to teach them. However, the Battalion Commander didn't want to lose his S4 at this critical time.

Because the Battalion Commander complained so much when he found out that General Wagstaff wanted me to personally teach the ARVN, the Brigade Commander told General Wagstaff that I had already trained the Brigade Training School on the use of mechanical ambushes, and asked if the school could teach the ARVN instead of me. Additionally, the Brigade Commander told General Wagstaff that I was now the Battalion S4, and with the upcoming stand down of the Battalion, I wouldn't have time to teach the ARVN and accomplish the mission of turning in the Battalion's weapons and equipment.

A few days later, General Wagstaff visited the Battalion forward area and asked the Battalion Commander, "What did you do with Schmidt?" The Battalion Commander just laughed because he was aware that the General already knew I was the S4. The General told my commander that he didn't realize that I had a new assignment prior to making the request for me to teach the Vietnamese forces in Binh Doung Province.

I respected Major General Wagstaff for his interest in what tactics were being used in the field at company level. He was the only general I met who visited any of my units in the field and asked for my opinion.

I would have liked to have trained more ARVN on the use of the mechanical ambush. However, I hope those who did receive the training were able to spread it throughout South Vietnam's military. It is likely that the mechanical ambush contributed to the success South Vietnam's military experienced in their counterinsurgency struggle prior to North Vietnam's 1975 invasion. Sadly, the mechanical ambush, while a great weapon to use against guerrilla fighters, is not very effective against large conventional infantry and armor units conducting a full scale attack. Against these units they needed US airpower.

Although I never gave any more classes to the ARVN, I did continue to provide classes on mechanical ambushes to various other US units within our area until I departed Vietnam in May of 1971. These classes not only taught the mechanics of the actual construction of the MA, but also included the tactical and operational concepts for their emplacement.

After leaving Vietnam in May of 1971, I taught the mechanical ambush only to United States Special Forces units and infantry units that I was assigned to (see figure 10). Returning from Vietnam I was assigned to the Army Infantry School at Fort Benning to attend the Infantry Advance Course. Because the course was not to start for two weeks the Tactics Committee tasked me to enter some of the more advanced techniques into the military's classified Booby Traps manual. Consequently, it would behoove all infantry officers to obtain a copy and study its contents.

CHAPTER 22

Part II Reflections

*The Lord said to Gideon, 'You have too many men for me
to deliver Midian into their hands. In order that Israel may
not boast against me that her own strength has saved her.'*

Judges 7:2[1]

To validate the importance of finding God's purpose for your life and
then living it, I started Part II of this book with information on how I
came to make the military my career. I believe the decision to surrender
my life to Jesus Christ resulted in not only God blessing my company in
Vietnam, but also a life full of joy, contentment, and true success (in God's
eyes) beyond my wildest dreams.

The intent of this book is not only to provide a warning about the
adverse consequences of disobedience to God and failing to acknowledge
our dependence on God's overruling power, but also to present evidence of
God's blessings on those who believe in Jesus Christ and motives are right.

It was God who provided Alpha Company with the wisdom to
establish an automated battlefield by studying the habits and patterns
of the enemy, then systematically employing mechanical ambushes. The
chronological events of Alpha Company from May to December of 1970
reveal how the use of a few mechanical ambushes on trails evolved into a
highly sophisticated and effective automated battlefield.

God truly blessed Alpha Company with success and protection. Alpha
Company killed or captured approximately sixty NVA/VC soldiers while

never losing any of their own men. This was a success not experienced by many (if any) other infantry companies in the Vietnam War.

A commander must always strive to accomplish the mission with minimal losses. They should treat each man as if he were his own son or brother. Sun Tzu said, "So a commander who advances not for glory, withdraws not to evade guilt, and cares for only the people's security along with the lord's interests is the country's treasure."[2]

Part II described how God used me to train South Vietnamese and other American troops in many of the effective techniques that Alpha Company developed. The use of the mechanical ambush was extremely effective as a counter guerrilla weapon, and probably contributed to South Vietnam's success in their counterinsurgency fight after America withdrew from Vietnam. However, it had little value against a conventional attack that consisted of large infantry and armor units.

Technology is always advancing; therefore, tactics should take advantage of it. In Vietnam, I tried to develop an automated battlefield that could keep my men out of harm's way whenever possible while still accomplishing the counter guerrilla mission. I envision that more and more unmanned weapon systems will be used in future wars. The current use of drones against our enemy and the use of improved anti-personnel landmines such as the XM-7 Spider Networked Munitions are two good examples. It is God who provides innovation for developing new systems and wisdom to effectively use them. We must do as Jesus tells us in Matthew 6:33: "seek first his kingdom and his righteousness, and all these things will be given to you as well."[3]

Therefore, even though the effective tactics and techniques identified in this book may not all work in future conflicts, the wisdom, insight, and intuition necessary to successfully accomplish future missions will always be available to those who follow the will of God and call upon the Lord Jesus Christ.

In light of the challenges our military will face in future wars, it is imperative for our leaders to trust in, pray to, and give thanks to the Lord for all things. 1 Thessalonians 5:17-18 states, "Be joyful always; pray continually; give thanks in all circumstances, for this is God's will for you in Christ Jesus."[4] Similarly, it is written in Philippians 4:6, "Do not be anxious about anything, but in everything, by prayer and petition, with thanksgiving, present your requests to God."[5]

However, it is important for America to understand, as individuals, and as a nation, what is written in James 5:16: "The prayer of a righteous man is powerful and effective."[6] Additionally, 1 John 5:14-15 says, "This is the confidence we have in approaching God: that if we ask anything according to his will, he hears us. And if we know that he hears us – whatever we ask – we know that we have what we asked of him."[7] If we expect God to answer our prayers, we must not only return to God, but ask for what is in God's will and not on worldly pleasures. The important and encouraging lesson from this verse is that each one of us can individually have a powerful effect on our nation through prayer. This verse also stresses the importance of electing people who are Christian and obedient to God to positions of authority within our government.

History shows that a nation's disobedience to God can result in its downfall. God loves his people; as a father disciplines his child, God will chastise us for our own good. However, when we are disciplined, we should learn from our mistake and repent. Hebrews 12:10–11, reminds us, "Our fathers disciplined us for a little while as they thought best; but God disciplines us for our good, that we may share in his holiness. No discipline seems pleasant at the time, but painful. Later on, however, it produces a harvest of righteousness and peace for those who have been trained by it."[8]

Where Do We Go from Here?

For God did not give us a spirit of timidity, but a spirit of power, of self-discipline.

2 Timothy 1:7[1]

As one who has been a soldier almost all my life so that the citizens of the United States and other nations can have the freedom to know Jesus Christ, it saddens me to see Vietnam only being allowed a highly controlled form of religious freedom. However, it saddens me even more to see the increasing number of Americans who have the freedom to read the Holy Bible, but are too busy to read it. Additionally, as shown in this book, failure to be obedient to God not only has adverse consequences for the nation in war, but also for all aspects of life. God's discipline is not limited to war, but includes natural disasters, crime, illegal drugs, plagues such as AIDs, economic breakdowns, terrorism, etc.

One can clearly see that there is not only a battle to be fought for freedom of religion around the world, but also a spiritual battle taking place within the United States. Ephesians 6:17, tells us that the sword of the Spirit to fight this battle against evil is the *word of God.*[2]

The Bible tells us that after fasting forty days and forty nights in the desert, the Devil tried to tempt Jesus to sin three times. Interestingly, the Devil sometimes used what was written in the Holy Scriptures out of context to tempt Jesus; however, each time Jesus quoted a Scripture that countered the Devil's scheme.[3]

At no other time in America's history have those in government so blatantly left the *word of God* out of their decisions. George Washington's 1789 unpublished letter to Congress which said, "The blessed Religion revealed in the Word of God will remain an eternal and awful monument to prove that the best institutions may be abused by human depravity; and that they may even, in some instances be made subservient to the vilest of purpose."[4]

I have never seen such unashamed disobedience to God from individuals in position of influence. Isaiah 5:20 provides the following warning for those responsible: "Woe to those who call evil good and good evil, who put darkness for light and light for darkness, who put bitter for sweet and sweet for bitter."[5]

Unfortunately, even some who say they are Christian call evil good and good evil because they have not read and studied the Holy Bible to find out what God considers sin. Therefore, Christian leaders must know what is written in the Holy Bible, believe it is the word of God and be obedient to it. America's leaders must understand the following verse from Psalm 81:13–14: "If my people would but listen to me (read the Bible), if Israel would follow my ways, how quickly would I subdue their enemies, and turn my hand against their foes!"[6]

When Abraham Lincoln was president, he was given a Bible as a gift. When he received the Holy Bible he said, "In regard to this Great Book, I have but to say. It is the best gift God has given to men. All the good the Savior gave to the world was communicated through this Book. But for it we could not know right from wrong."[7] Not knowing what is written in the Bible is to fight our nation's spiritual battle without a weapon. Although I believe most Americans still believe the Bible is the word of God, I think only a few actually have read and studied it to know what the Bible says about various important issues. Many Americans who profess to be Christians and have the freedom to read and learn what is written in the Bible seem to be too preoccupied with making money and pleasing themselves to want to know God and learn what pleases Him. Can we as a nation, therefore, expect God's blessings?

The Lord allowed my company to achieve victory; however, He denied victory to the nation. I truly believe the Holy Bible is God's word and God has demonstrated to me that He is faithful to what is written in the Bible.

For over two hundred years our nation has considered the Holy Bible the word of God and our moral compass. Unfortunately, since the sixties, much of our nation has lost its moral compass, and if the United States expects to be blessed by God, its people must return to the Holy Bible. It is written in Joshua 1:8, "Do not let this Book of the Law depart from your mouth; meditate on it day and night, so that you may be careful to do everything written in it. Then you will be prosperous and successful."[8]

Although Christians have victory over death through Jesus Christ, God calls us to bring others to Him. The following paragraphs from Matthew 5:14-16 call Christians to action: "You are the light of the world. A city on a hill cannot be hidden. Neither do people light a lamp and put it under a bowl. Instead they put it on its stand, and it gives light to everyone in the house. In the same way, let your light shine before men, that they may see your good deeds and praise your Father in heaven."[9]

Because in the past almost all of the United States' citizens were Christian, God blessed the United States and it became the light of the world, "A city on a hill." However, as the United States' citizens continues to fall away from Christ, its light is becoming dimmer. In Romans 2:23-24 Paul says to the Jews living in Rome, "You who brag about the law, do you dishonor God by breaking the law? As it is written: 'God's name is blasphemed among the Gentiles because of you.'"[10] Similar to this verse about the Jews written almost 2000 years ago, because of the immoral behavior of many Americans today, Jesus Christ's name is dishonored and blasphemed, rather than praised, around the world by those who still think America is all true Christians.

In Old Testament times, God blessed Israel to show the world that they worshiped the one true God. Likewise, I believe God has made the United States the most blessed nation in world to show the world that we believe in and worship the one true God – Jesus Christ. However, if faith in Jesus Christ and obedience to Him is no longer considered a primary characteristic of the United States, why should God continue to bless our nation?

This book suggest that the defeat in Vietnam was God disciplining the United States so that its' citizens would repent and return to Him. Since the citizens in the United States that do not believe in Jesus as their savior do not have the light, we Christians who have the light must light-up the nation. We Christians must increase our efforts to spread the Gospel of

Jesus Christ within the United States and to also take a more active role in America's government, policies, and the education of our youth. Jesus tells us above in Matthew 5:14 that Christians are the light of the world and we should not put our light under a bowl, but rather let it give light to everyone.

Certainly, we who genuinely believe that Jesus is our Lord and Savior will receive eternal life; however, Christians are also called to become more like Jesus and to bring glory and honor to God. Each of us has been given specific gifts to accomplish God's purpose. Because God loves us, He also disciplines us Christians when we fail to do His will.

It is important to note that the verse quoted below does not guarantee that God works good for all that call themselves Christians; he only does for those who love God and who have been called according to God's purpose. Romans 8:28 states, "And we know that in all things God works for the good of those who love him, who have been called according to his purpose."[11]

This verse is certainly comforting, but how does a Christian know that he loves God enough to qualify as one of the people in which the above verse applies? Jesus' answer to this question is provided in John 14:23–24, "If anyone loves me, he will obey my teaching. My Father will love him, and we will come to him and make our home with him. He who does not love me will not obey my teaching. These words you hear are not my own; they belong to the Father who sent me."[12] If we love Jesus and want to obey His teachings, we must find out what they are.

Ephesians 5:8–10 says, "For you were once darkness, but now you are light in the Lord. Live as children of light (for the fruit of the light consists in all goodness, righteousness and truth) and ***find out what pleases the Lord.***"[13]

The only place we can find Jesus' teaching is from the New Testament of the Holy Bible; therefore, those who truly love God should have a desire to read and study the Bible.

It is my experience that when I ask people within the United States what God's position is on current issues clearly identified in the Bible as sin, such as greed, revenge, coveting, homosexuality, fornication (sex outside of marriage), drunkenness, killing God-created children developing in the womb, etc., many either do not know or do not care. Basing our values and morals on our own sinful human nature and shallow human understanding rather than finding out what the Lord desires is a major reason for our nation's decline. Can America really say "In God We Trust" when we believe and follow our simple human (so called) logic, understanding, and wisdom over what God's Holy Word tells us? The Bible tells us in Proverbs 3:5, "Trust in the Lord with all your heart and lean not on your own understanding."[14]

There are a number of people who claim to be Christian and who know what is written in the Bible, but lack a strong enough faith to believe that the whole Bible is the word of God. These people tend to only believe those parts of the Bible that satisfy their own human desires and limited human reasoning. Second Timothy 3:16-17 clearly states, "All Scripture is God-breathed and is useful for teaching, rebuking, correcting and training in righteousness, so that the man of God may be thoroughly equipped for every good work."[15]

Saint Paul explains why some do not believe the Bible in his letter to the Christian church of Corinth which states, "We have not received the spirit of the world but the Spirit who is from God, that we may understand what God has freely given us. That is what we speak, not in words taught us by human wisdom, but in words taught by the Spirit, expressing spiritual truths in spiritual words. The man without the Spirit does not accept the things that come from the Spirit of God, for they are foolishness to him, and he cannot understand them, because they are spiritually discerned. The spiritual man makes judgments about all things, but he himself is not subject to any man's judgment: 'For who has known the mind of the Lord that he may instruct him?' But we have the mind of Christ."[16]

Saint Paul also provided us the following prophetic warning in 2 Timothy 4:3: "For the time will come when men will not put up with sound doctrine. Instead, to suit their own desires, they will gather around them a great number of teachers to say what their itching ears want to hear."[17]

I would remind those who claim the commands given within the New Testament no longer apply today and call those who do "dinosaurs" that Hebrews 13:8 states, "Jesus Christ is the same yesterday and today and forever."[18] Jesus Christ said in Matthew 5:18, "I tell you the truth, until heaven and earth disappear, not the smallest letter, not the least stroke of a pen, will by any means disappear from the Law until everything is accomplished."[19]

In light of the fact that Jesus has not changed, America needs to revisit our current morals and positions on issues that the Bible clearly identifies as sin. Christians must take an active role in changing the current laws of America that allow the entertainment, media, and government to promote these immoral acts.

In a democracy the most effective way to accomplish the above is through the ballot box. However, those that are knowledgeable of what is written in the Bible should also boldly quote the specific verses that address the various moral issues to others. This should be done in a loving and respectful manner. It is important to make it clear that we are all sinners and you are not being judgmental, but only saying what is written in the Bible.

To bring others to Christ we Christians must study the Bible so that we can do what Saint Peter tells us to do in 1 Peter 3:13-15, "Who is going to harm you if you are eager to do good? But even if you should suffer for what is right, you are blessed. Do not fear what they fear; do not be frightened. But in your hearts set apart Christ as Lord. Always be prepared to give an answer to everyone who asks you to give the reason for the hope that you have. But do this with gentleness and respect."[20] The hope Peter is referring to is our salvation in Jesus Christ; however, I believe we can apply his advice to all biblical teaching.

In particular, those who are in positions of influence, such as teachers, pastors, radio and TV announcers, movie and TV producers, celebrities, and various leaders, should have the courage to quote what is written in the Bible. The half-brother of Jesus says in James 3:1, "Not many of you should presume to be teachers, my brothers, because you know that we who teach will be judged more strictly."[21] Jesus says in Matthew 5:19, "Anyone who breaks one of the least of these commandments and teaches others to do the same will be called least in the kingdom of heaven, but whoever practices and teaches these commands will be called great in the kingdom of heaven."[22]

Certainly, the Gospel of Jesus Christ and God's grace are the most important messages; however, the Bible was written also to inform us what pleases the Lord and what God identifies as immoral. When Jesus said to "make disciples of all nations," He not only said to baptize them in the name of the Father, the Son, and Holy Spirit, but also said to teach them to obey everything He had commanded.

Paul tells us that those who believe in the Gospel of Jesus Christ have eternal life; however, what a person's eternal reward is when he arrives in heaven depends on the quality (in God's sight) of his works done in this life. First Corinthians 3:12-15 states, "If any man builds on this foundation (faith in the Gospel of Jesus) using gold, silver, costly stones, wood, hay or straw, his work will be revealed with fire, and the fire will test the quality of each man's work. If what he has built survives, he will receive his reward. If it is burned up, he will suffer loss, he himself will be saved, but only as one escaping through the flames."[23]

This book shows that the war in Vietnam was winnable and then provided the answer to why the US failed to win a lasting victory in the Vietnam War. Many other authors have identified mistakes made by the US in the Vietnam War; however, because they fail to mention man's dependence on the overruling power of God, they have never identified why God allowed the mistakes. Consequently, their conclusions provide little help at preventing America from future disasters.

It is important to study military concepts; however, it is God who provides wisdom, intuition, and creativity. It is God who allows even the circumstances that lead to war and God who determines who wins the war. Therefore, the first and most important question in a study of the Vietnam War is - why **did God allow** the US to fail? This book has presented a case that supports the theory that God was disciplining the US for its immorality so that its citizens would correct their behavior and return to God.

Today America is in a spiritual war, more dangerous than a war fought with bullets and bombs. Just as a soldier would not have been effective in Vietnam without his M-16, we cannot be effective in this spiritual battle without a weapon, which in this spiritual battle is the word of God.

Therefore, for the United States as a nation to be blessed, Christians within America must know what is written in the Bible and actively spread the Gospel so that our citizens will believe that Jesus Christ is their Lord and Savior. Additionally, Christians must encourage others within the United States to love God and their fellow man, and return to the Holy Bible as their moral compass.

NOTES

Introduction

1   Proverbs 21:31, *The Holy Bible (NIV)*.
2   Proverbs 13:18, *The Holy Bible (NIV)*.
3   Proverbs 1:7, *The Holy Bible (NIV)*

Part I
Chapter I

1   Psalm 81:13-14, *The Holy Bible (NIV)*.
2   Proverbs 21:31, *The Holy Bible (NIV)*.
3   Leviticus 26:17-18, *The Holy Bible (NIV)*.
4   1 Corinthians 10:11, *The Holy Bible (NIV)*.
5   Harry G. Summers, Jr., *On Strategy: The Vietnam War in Context* (Strategic Studies Institute U.S. Army War College,1981),1.
6   H.R. McMasters, "Dereliction of Duty," (Harper Perennial, 1998).
7   William C. Westmoreland, General, U.S.A., "Vietnam in Perspective," *Military Review*, January 1979, 38-39.

Chapter 2

1   Hebrew 11:30, *The Holy Bible (NIV)*.
2   Matthew 5:43-45, *The Holy Bible (NIV)*.
3   R.M. Shoemaker, General, US Army, "Dealing with a Just War" (Insert to letter, Headquarters, US Army Forces Command, January 29, 1982).
4   Ibid.
5   James E. Schmidt, Lieutenant Colonel, US Army Special Forces, "Hit Drug Lords' Center of Gravity," *Army Magazine*, July 1992, 18–23.
6   Matthew 8:10, *The Holy Bible, (NIV)*.
7   Luke 3:14, *The Holy Bible, (NIV)*.

8   Acts 10, *The Holy Bible (NIV)*
9   Peter A. Lillback, *George Washington's Sacred Fire* (Providence: Forum Press, 2006), 574–575.
10 Samuel 17:49–52, *The Holy Bible, (NIV)*.
11 Abraham Lincoln, in K. McDowell Beliles, *America's Providential History*, 225-26.
12 David W. Balsiger, Joette Whims, Melody Hunskor, *The Incredible Power of Prayer*, (Wheaton, Illinois: Tyndale House, 1998), 285.
13 Carl von Clausewitz, *On War*, edited and translated by Michael Howard and Peter Paret with Introductory Essays by Peter Paret, Michael Howard, and Bernard Brodie and a Commentary by Bernard Brodie (Princeton: Princeton UP, 1976), III:3, 185.
14 James 1:5, *The Holy Bible (NIV)*. 1 Kings 3:12, *The Holy Bible (NIV)*.
15 1 Kings 3:12, *The Holy Bible (NIV)*.
16 Robert S. McNamara, *In Retrospect: the Tragedy and Lessons of Vietnam* (New York: Times Books, 1995), 313.

Chapter 3

1   Proverbs 9:10. *The Holy Bible (NIV)*.
2   Department of the Army, "The Principles of War," *Operations Manual 100-5*, B-1.
3   Department of the Army, *Counterinsurgency Field Manual 3-24*, June 2006, 1–16.

Chapter 4

1   Dave Richard Palmer, Brigadier General., U.S.A, *Summons of the Trumpet: US-Vietnam in Perspective* (San Rafael, California: Presidio, 1978), 75.
2   Department of Defense, *Joint Publication 1-02*.
3   Clausewitz, *On War*, VIII:4, 595–596.
4   Richard Nixon, *The Real War* (Warner Books Inc., 1980), 307.
5   Clausewitz, *On War*, VIII: 4, 595–596.
6   Lewis Sorley, *A Better War* (Harcourt: 1999), 29.

Chapter 5

1   Proverbs 1:29–32. *The Holy Bible, (NIV)*.
2   Proverbs 15:22. *The Holy Bible, (NIV)*.
3   Harold G. Moore and Joseph L. Galloway, *We are Solders Still: A Journey Back to the Battlefields of Vietnam* (HarperCollins, 2008), 5–13.

4   Ibid., 122–123.

5   Sorley, *A Better War*, 184.

6   Ibid., 140.

7   George C. Wilson, *Mud Soldiers: Life Inside the New American Army* (New York: Scribner, 1989), 38–39.

8   Sun Tzu, *The Art of War* translated and edited by J.H. Huang (New York: HarperCollins, 2008), 67.

9   Ibid., 40–41.

10 David Maraniss, *They Marched into Sunlight: War and Peace, Vietnam and America, October 1967* (S&S, 2004), 217.

11 Ibid., 314 and 341–342.

12 Ibid., 260–261.

Chapter 6

1   Harold G. Moore and Joseph L. Galloway, *We Are Soldiers Still: A Journey Back to the Battlefields of Vietnam* (New York: HarperCollins, 2009), 122–123.

2   Maraniss, *They Marched into Sunlight: War and Peace, Vietnam and America, October 1967*, 217.

3   Moore and Galloway, *We Are Soldiers Still: A Journey Back to the Battlefields of Vietnam*, 122.

4   Ibid., 123.

5   Wilson, *Mud Soldiers: Life inside the new American Army*, 38–39.

6   John S. Bowman, *The Vietnam War: An Almanac* (Bison, 1985), 167.

7   Ibid., 170.

8   Ibid., 171.

9   Ibid.,172.

10 Ibid., 173.

11 Ibid., 173.

12 Ibid., 174.

13 Ibid., 174.

14 Ibid., 174.

15 Ibid., 174.

16 Ibid., 180.

17 Maraniss, *They Marched into Sunlight: War and Peace, Vietnam and America, October 1967*,217.

18 Bowman, *The Vietnam War: An Almanac*, 189.

19 Ibid., 198.

20 Sorley, *A Better War*, 36.

21 Bowman, *The Vietnam War: An Almanac*, 235.

22 Ibid., 241.

23 Ibid., 250.

24 Ibid., 250.

Chapter 7

1 Sun Tzu, *The Art of War*, translated and with an introduction by Samuel B. Griffith (OUP, 1963), 43.

2 Department of the Army, *Field Manual 6-20, p. D-5.*

3 Ibid., D-4.

4 John E. O'Neill and Jerome R. Corsi, Ph.D., *Unfit for Command* (Regnery, 2004), 53.

5 Sun Tzu, *The Art of War*, 71.

Chapter 8

1 Lewis Sorley, *A Better War*, 374.

2 Nixon, *The Real War*, 119.

Chapter 9

1 2 Chronicles 7:14, *The Holy Bible, (NIV).*

2 Sun Tzu, *The Art of War*, 41.

Part II
Chapter 10

1 General MacArthur, "Farewell Speech to Congress."(April 19, 1951).

2 Charles Stanley, *Success God's Way* (Thomas Nelson, 2000).

3 Rick Warren, *The Purpose Driven Life*, (Zondervan, 2002)

4 4. Ephesians 2:8–10, *The Holy Bible (NIV).*

5 United Nations General Assembly, "The Universal Declaration of Human Rights" (December 10, 1948).

6 Mark 8:38, *The Holy Bible (NIV).*

7 James 4:17, *The Holy Bible, (NIV).*

8 Matthew 25:14–30, *The Holy Bible (NIV).*

9 Matthew 10:38-39, *The Holy Bible (NIV).*

10 Philippians 4:13, *The Holy Bible (NIV).*

Chapter 11

1 Proverbs 1:33, *The Holy Bible, (NIV)*.
2 Sun Tzu, *The Art of War*, 57.

Chapter 12

1 Psalm 23:1–4, *The Holy Bible (NIV)*.
2 Keith William Nolan, *Into Cambodia: Spring Campaign, Summer Offensive, 1970* (Presidio, 1990), 296.
3 Sun Tzu, *The Art of War*, 57.
4 Ibid., 74.
5 Psalms 91:14, *The Holy Bible (NIV)*.

Chapter 13

1 Matthew 6:33, *The Holy Bible (NIV)*.
2 1 John 5:14-15, *The Holy Bible (NIV)*.
3 Proverbs 16:3, *The Holy Bible (NIV)*.
4 1 Peter 5:9, *The Holy Bible (NIV)*.
5 Romans 8:24, *The Holy Bible (NIV)*.
6 Act 7:54-60, *The Holy Bible (NIV)*.
7 Mark 8:38, *The Holy Bible (NIV)*.
8 Ephesians 2:8-9, *The Holy Bible (NIV)*.
9 Luke 6:22-23, *The Holy Bible (NIV)*.
10 John 9:3, *The Holy Bible (NIV)*.
11 Job 42:7, *The Holy Bible (NIV)*.
12 Proverbs 3:5, *The holy Bible (NIV)*.
13 1 Peter 1:3-7, *The Holy Bible (NIV)*.
14 Matthew 10:33, *The Holy Bible (NIV)*.
15 2 Corinthians 12:8, *The Holy Bible (NIV)*.
16 Philippians 3:19-21, *The Holy Bible (NIV)*.
17 1 Corinthians 13:3, *The Holy Bible (NIV)*.

Chapter 14

1 Proverbs 2:6–8, *The Holy Bible, (NIV)*.
2 Clausewitz, On War, VI:1, 358.
3 Sun Tzu, The Art of War, 63.
4 Sun Tzu, The Art of War, 43.

Chapter 15

1 Psalm 118:6, *The Holy Bible (NIV)*.
2 Department of the Army, "Military Leadership," *Field Manual 22-100*, 1.
3 Psalm 115:9, *The Holy Bible (NIV)*.

Chapter 16

1 Joshua 1:7, *The Holy Bible (NIV)*.
2 James 4:2–3, *The Holy Bible (NIV)*.
3 Sun Tzu, *The Art of War*, 40–41.

Chapter 17

1 Psalms 91:4–5, *The Holy Bible (NIV)*.
2 Maraniss, *They Marched into Sunlight: War and Peace, Vietnam and America, October 1967*, 410.

Chapter 18

1 2 Chronicles 20:15, *The Holy Bible (NIV)*.
2 1 Kings 6:16, *The Holy Bible (NIV)*.
3 1 Samuel 17:37, *The Holy Bible (NIV)*.

Chapter 19

1 Joshua 23:9–11, *The Holy Bible, (NIV)*.
2 John 14:5-6, *The Holy Bible, (NIV)*.
3 Nolan, *Into Cambodia: Spring Campaign, Summer Offensive, 1970*, 407.
4 Department of the Army, "Military Leadership," *Field Manual 22-100*, 69–70.

Chapter 20

1 Joshua 1:5, *The Holy Bible (NIV)*.

Chapter 21

1 Ephesians 3:20, *The Holy Bible (NIV)*.

Chapter 22

1 Judges 7:2, *The Holy Bible (NIV)*.

2 Sun Tzu, *The Art of War*, 92.

3 Matthew 6:33, *The Holy Bible (NIV)*.

4 1 Thessalonians 5:16–18, *The Holy Bible (NIV)*.

5 Philippians 4:6, *The Holy Bible (NIV)*.

6 James 5:16, *The Holy Bible (NIV)*.

7 1 John 5:14-15, *The Holy Bible (NIV)*.

8 Hebrews 12:10–11, *The Holy Bible (NIV)*.

Epilogue

1 2 Timothy 1:7, *The Holy Bible (NIV)*.

2 Ephesians 6:17, *The Holy Bible (NIV)*.

3 Matthew 4:2-3, *The Holy Bible (NIV)*.

4 *Lillback, George Washington's Sacred Fire*, 564.

5 Isaiah 5:20, *The Holy Bible (NIV)*.

6 Psalm 81:13–14, *The Holy Bible (NIV)*.

7 Dr. Jerry Newcombe, *The Way Out: God's Solution to Moral Chaos in America*, DVD, (Truth In Action Ministries, 2011).

8 Joshua 1:8, *The Holy Bible (NIV)*.

9 Matthew 5:14–16, *The Holy Bible (NIV)*.

10 Romans 2:23-24, *The Holy Bible (NIV)*.

11 Romans 8:28, *The Holy Bible (NIV)*.

12 John 14:23–24, *The Holy Bible (NIV)*.

13 Ephesians 5:8-10, *The Holy Bible (NIV)*.

14 Proverbs 3:5, *The Holy Bible (NIV)*.

15 2 Timothy 3:16–17, *The Holy Bible (NIV)*.

16 1 Corinthians 2:12–16, *The Holy Bible (NIV)*.

17 2 Timothy 4:3, *The Holy Bible (NIV)*.

18 Hebrews 13:8, *The Holy Bible (NIV)*.

19 Matthew 5:18, *The Holy Bible (NIV)*.

20 1 Peter 3:13-15, *The Holy Bible (NIV)*.

21 James 3:1, *The Holy Bible (NIV)*.

22 Matthew 5:19, *The Holy Bible (NIV)*.

23 1 Corinthians 3:12-15, *The Holy Bible (NIV)*.

LTC Schmidt holds a Bachelor of Science degree in business form Southeast Missouri State College and an MBA from the University of Missouri. Jim and his wife, Joyce, live in Fort Collins, Colorado, and have two grown daughters, a grown son, and nine grandchildren.

Jim is also the author of the 2012 book "Victory Rests with the Lord: God in the Vietnam War."

GLOSSARY OF ACRONYMS AND DEFINITIONS

ARVN: Army of the Republic of Vietnam (South Vietnamese Army)

AO: area of operation

APC: Armored Personnel Carrier

AVLB: Armored Vehicle Launched Bridge

Canister round: anti-personnel round fired out of a tank. (Rather than the tank firing an anti-tank or high explosive round it can fire a canister round which consists of a thousand steel balls)

CHICOM: Chinese Communist

CHICOM Claymore: Communist enemy anti-personnel mine

CIA: Central Intelligence Agency (U.S.)

CIDG: Civilian Irregular Defense Group (South Vietnamese nationals recruited in remote areas to operate with U.S. Army Special Forces)

CINCPAC: commander-in-chief, Pacific (U.S. unified commander of Pacific Command (PACOM) which includes all American forces in the Pacific Theater, including Southeast Asia)

Conventional Infantry unit: approximately 800 men in a battalion, 200 men in a company, 40 men in a platoon.

Cordon: encircle a village to keep enemy soldiers from escaping

CORDS: Civil Operations and Revolutionary Development Support

COSVN: Central Office for South Vietnam (the senior headquarters used by the North Vietnamese communist party for political and military control of its organization in South Vietnam)

Claymore: U.S. claymore is an anti-personnel mine (M-18A1). (Contains C-4 explosive behind a matrix of about 700 1/8-inch steel balls. When detonated, it propels these 700 balls in a 60-degree fan-shaped pattern up to 100 meters)

DMZ: demilitarized zone (created by the Geneva Accords of 1954 along the 17th parallel dividing South and North Vietnam)

Flechette round: an artillery, tank, air-to-ground missile, or recoilless rifle round that consists of a thousand small dart-shaped projectiles. (It is used against personnel in the open and sometimes referred to as a beehive round)

Free-Fire Zone: in Vietnam it meant that a soldier was authorized to fire at any person who could be identified as an enemy soldier without having permission from a higher headquarters.

FSB: fire support base (base from where artillery is fired from)

HQ: headquarters

JCS: Joint Chiefs of Staff (U.S.)

KIA: Killed In Action

Laager: a mechanized infantry or armor unit's night defensive position

Leg Infantry: In Vietnam they walked or were airlifted (airmobile) compared to mechanized infantry which use armored personnel carriers (APCs)

LP: listening post (used to detect enemy movement at night)

LRRP: Long Range Reconnaissance Patrol (small 4-5 man unit)

LZ: Landing Zone

MACV: Military Assistance Command, Vietnam (U.S.)

MA: Mechanical Ambush

NDP: night defensive position

NLF: National Liberation Front (principal Viet Cong command center for guerrilla operations in South Vietnam)

NVA: North Vietnamese Army

OP: observation post (used to detect enemy movement during day light)

OPSEC: operational security

PZ: Pickup Zone

Restricted AO: no one can enter or fire into the designated Area of Operation unless the commander assigned the Restricted AO is notified. (anyone in a "Restricted AO" without permission is assumed enemy)

RPG: Russian "Hand-held Anti-Tank Grenade Launcher." RPG is the

Russian acronym of "Ruchnoy Protivotankoviy Granstomyot." However, most English speakers believe RPG stands for "Rocket-Propelled Grenade."

SAM: surface-to-air missile

SOCPAC: Special Operations Command, Pacific

TRP: Target Reference Point (a numbered point on the map that immediate artillery or mortars can fire)

USAF: U.S. Air Force

USARV: U.S. Army, Vietnam

VC: Viet Cong (South Vietnam communists)

WIA: Wounded In Action

Printed in the United States
by Baker & Taylor Publisher Services